RHYMES AND RECOLLECTIONS

OF

A HAND-LOOM WEAVER.

Willie joins me in regards to all — Yours ever truly

June 1845

W Thom

RHYMES AND RECOLLECTIONS

OF

A HAND-LOOM WEAVER.

BY WILLIAM THOM,
OF
INVERURY.

"An' syne whan nichts grew cauld an' lang,
Ae while he sicht — ae while he sang."
Old Ballad.

THIRD EDITION,
WITH ADDITIONS.

LONDON:
SMITH, ELDER AND CO., 65, CORNHILL.

1847.

THIS BOOK IS PRESENTED

TO

EMMA KATHARINE GORDON,

LADY OF KNOCKESPOCK,

BY

The Author,

WHO HAD THE HAPPINESS FOR A TIME TO BE A SHARER

IN THE GENERAL GLADNESS OF HER HOME;

WHERE MANY, AS WELL AS HE, REGRET

SHE LEAVES WHEN AUTUMN WEARY
BIDS WINTER WASTE THE PLAIN;
SHE LOOKS ON LANDS MAIR CHEARY,
'TIL OURS ARE GREEN AGAIN.

OH, WOULD SHE DWELL AMONG US
WHEN DALES ARE DEEP WI' SNAW,
DOUR WINTER COULD NA WRANG US,
NOR SIMMER SEEM AWA'.

KNOCKESPOCK,
September, 1844.

CONTENTS.

	Page
* DEDICATION TO MRS. GORDON, OF KNOCKESPOCK.	
TO THE READER	1
* PREFACE TO THE SECOND EDITION . . .	5
* RECOLLECTIONS	7
DITTO	21
DITTO	39
THE BLIND BOY'S PRANKS, NO. I. . . .	53
" " " NO. II. . . .	57
" " " NO. III. . . .	63
* LINES OCCASIONED BY THE SUDDEN DEATH OF COUNT JOHN LESLIE OF BALQUHAIN AND FETTERNEIR	67
* WHISPERINGS FOR THE UNWASHED . . .	72
THE MANIAC MOTHER'S DREAM . . .	77
OLD FATHER FROST AND HIS FAMILY . . .	84
AUTUMN WINDS	89
OH, MARY! WHEN YOU THINK OF ME . .	91
I'VE SOUGHT IN LANDS AYONT THE SEA . .	93
I WOULDNA—OH! I COULDNA LOOK . .	95
JEANIE'S GRAVE	97
THEY SPEAK O' WYLES	99
THE LAST TRYST	100
ONE OF THE HEART'S STRUGGLES . . .	102
YE DINNA KEN YON BOWER	104

* Not in First Edition.

CONTENTS.

	Page
BONNIE MAY	106
LINES WRITTEN AT RAVENSCRAIG	108
A LETTER TO THE EDITOR OF THE ———	110
THE OVERGATE OF DUNDEE ORPHAN	112
YTHANSIDE	114
A CHIEFTAIN UNKNOWN TO THE QUEEN	117
THE DRUNKARD'S DREAM	119
CAN YE FORGET?	121
THE LASS O' KINTORE	123
DID THEY MEET AGAIN?	125
THE LASS WI' THE WANDERIN' E'E	127
MY HEATHER LAND	129
MY HAMELESS HA'	131
LETTER TO J. ROBERTSON, ESQ.	133
TO MY SON WILLIE	134
" IN THE INFIRMARY	136
DREAMINGS OF THE BEREAVED	138
THE MITHERLESS BAIRN	140
THE WEDDED WATERS	142
OH, THAT MY LOVE WAS SO EASILY WON!	144
SECOND LOVE	146
ADDRESS TO THE DON	147
* WHISPER LOW	150
* GLAMOURIE; OR, MESMERISM AS WE HAVE IT AT INVERURY	152
* SCHOOL OF INDUSTRY, ABERDEEN	155
* MONITOR'S SONG	156
* THE STRICKEN BRANCH	159
* THE FISHERMEN	162
* LINES SUGGESTED BY THE ABOVE DISASTER	164
* LINES TO MISS LUCY LAWRENCE OTTLEY	166
KNOCKESPOCK'S LADY (ADDITIONAL STANZAS)	168
NOTES, (BY ANOTHER HAND)	173
INDEX OF PERSONS AND PLACES	185
THE AUTHOR'S ACKNOWLEDGMENT	191

* Not in First Edition.

TO THE READER.

If, in my song or in my saying, there appears more of Egotism than enough, how can I avoid it and speak at all? The narrative portion of these pages is a record of scenes and circumstances interwoven with my experience—with my destiny. Hence the necessity of my telling my own tale. Then the feelings and fancies, the pleasure and the pain, that for a time hovered about my aimless existence were all my own—my property. These aërial investments I held and fashioned into measured verse.

Thus, by the self-derived authority whereby I tell my own tale, do I sing my own song; so that *I*, *We*, and *Us*, are the all and all of the matter. The self-portraiture herein attempted is not altogether Egotism neither, inasmuch as the main lineaments of the sketch are to be found in the separate histories of a thousand families in Scotland within these last ten years. That fact, however, being contemplated in mass, and in reference to its bulk only, acts more on the *wonder* than on the *pity* of mankind, as if human sympathies, like the human eye, could not compass an object exceedingly large, and same time exceedingly near. It is no small share in the end and aim of the present little work, to impart to one portion of the community a glimpse of what is sometimes going on in another; and even if only *that* is accomplished, some good service will be done. I have long had a notion that many of the heartburnings that run through the SOCIAL WHOLE, spring, not so much from the distinctiveness of classes, as their mutual ignorance of each other. The miserably rich look on the miserably poor with distrust and dread, scarcely giving them credit for sensibility sufficient to feel their own sorrows. That is ignorance with its gilded side. The poor, in turn, foster a hatred of the wealthy as a sole inheritance—look on grandeur as their natural enemy, and bend to the rich man's rule in gall and bleeding scorn. Shallows on the one side, and Demagogues on the other, are the portions that come oftenest into contact. These are the luckless things that skirt the great divisions, exchanging all that is offensive therein. "MAN KNOW THYSELF" should be written on the right hand; on the left, "MEN KNOW EACH OTHER." It is a subject worthy of a wise head and a pithy pen.

To these I leave it, and turn to tell my readers a few words more about this book.

With very little exception, everything here presented was written in Inverury, and within these last three years. The "Recollections" are introduced for the sake of the "Rhymes," and in the same relationship as parent and child—one the offspring of the other; and in that association alone can they be interesting. I write no more in either than what I knew—and not all of that—so Feeling has left Fancy little to do in the matter.

PREFACE

TO

THE SECOND EDITION.

Some degree of Fancy has fallen to my lot,—Judgment, in the better construction of the term, has been to me but sparingly doled out,—so, instead of building up a preface to my second edition in the ordinary thanksgivings to "gentle readers" and "discerning publics," I *fancy* it will serve as well, be as useful, to take a step "back-lan's," as we say in the North, and cut *in* a portion of recollections bearing on sundry matters previous to my settlement at Newtyle, in Forfarshire.

I have read in some book, but I forget where, that *every* body has much in his life and fortunes worth knowing; none in which a careful gleaner may not find something that will repay his notice. It must be so; since life itself is but a lesson, long or short, smooth or rough, as may be; and never was any one so dogged and dull but it taught him something different to all it taught to others. As there are not two human visages alike in every feature, so neither will be found two human destinies in every way alike. The lightest atom that floats in air will have its influence on man and kingdoms,—what wonder, then, if we differ in taste, in loving and in loathing, in brown hair or in black, in apparel to the body as in religion to the soul. We are governed by unsought visitants from earth, air, and sea, and by influences from each other; and what we call "*Will*" is no more than the fact of our yielding to these influences; but when these visitants find no fastening and pass away, we bravely pride ourselves on sin resisted!

RECOLLECTIONS.

Among the many stately buildings that now claim a stranger's notice as he approaches Aberdeen from the south, most of all will he admire the cluster of churches lately erected at the north end of Belmont Street. The change is grateful even to the eye, when one remembers the odious looking "*rickles*" that for seventy long years disfigured that spot. How much more beautiful, and how emphatic the contrast in another and dearer light, to those who know the misery, the destroying influences, that during nearly a century were upheld and nourished within the dismal walls of the "School Hill Factory"—there, as once it stood, a prime nursery of vice and sorrow. Many, many a miserable wanderer in after years, of unrevealed suffering and bitter penitence could date that doom from the hour yon blue gates shut upon him. Virtue perished within its walls—utterly perished, and was dreamed of no more; or, if remembered at all, only in a deep and woful sense of self-debasement—a struggling to forget, where it was hopeless to obtain. So Folly, Sin, and Shame stalked abroad from this grand nursery unheeded. Never mind that, it was a most "thriving concern" to its owners. It is a duty, do it who may—and it shall be done—to expose the factory system of that day, as it stood in our "moral North." Fairly to put the knife into the dead monster, lay bare its dark core, dissect it in broad day, that the world may see who had the fat and who the famine portion of that heartless trading. Then weep the folly of seeking beyond the ocean for that sin and slavery we had so rife at home. Meantime, here is offered only an undetailed view of the main elements, forbearing at present to trace their livelong influences on myself and others. True, the rubbishly stain is blotted from the earth—not so the evils it reared, and cast upon society. Nor are all its ancient tenants in the dust. At every turning of my native city, I meet the shadow of a former shopmate, haggard, and prematurely old, worn beyond the pale of usefulness on earth, sunken, perishing.

God speed yon holy buildings, be they kirks Free or Fast. There they are instead of an olden-time factory; and that it is so, the best wish that the best heart can form, the wish will be, that the new building become the means of rescuing as many souls as the evil tutory of its predecessor has sent astray.

About the year 1770 this work commenced, experimenting on a small way the jenny-spinning, then but lately discovered. After some time other houses were added, and the whole converted into one entire weaving factory: the company, a powerful one, having erected an extensive spinning-mill at Woodside, close by Aberdeen. Then was the daisy portion of weaving—the bright and mid-day period of all who pitched a shuttle, and of the happy one whose luck it was to win a weaver's smile. Four days did the weaver work,—for then four days was a week, as far as working went,—and such a week to a skilful workman brought forty shillings. Sunday, Monday, and Tuesday, were of course jubilee. Lawn frills gorged freely from under the wrists of his fine blue, gilt-buttoned coat. He dusted his head with white flour on Sunday, smirked, and wore a cane. Walked in clean slippers on Monday—Tuesday heard him talk war bravado, quote Volney, and get drunk. Weaving commenced gradually on Wednesday: then were little children pirn-fillers, and such were taught to steal warily past the gate-keeper, concealing the bottle. These "wee" smugglers had a drop for their services,* over and beyond their chances of profiting by the elegant and edifying

* They know little of the matter who know only the physical evils bred in factories.

discussions uttered in their hearing. Infidelity was just then getting fashionable. When I first became an inmate of this building in 1814, only two or three veteran fools lived to feel the deplorable change that had overtaken our helpless calling, and to witness the more deplorable continuance and extending of habits begun and fostered by them in years of fulness, yet still clinging to the lean frame and torn doublet of the tenpence-a-day weaver, and imparted by him to the green-horns around. What could not now be done in full, was imitated pretty well; and, if money was absent, device was ever near. Many curious expedients were weekly discovered, and as duly practised. To raise the wind-convivial; to keep it breezing, when raised, secured distinction and approval.

Be the graceless details forgotten!—I can only allude to these desperate and ingenious resources as answering the questions—" How could dissipation exist where wages barely afforded ordinary sustenance?" It was so—the weaver of forty shillings bequeathed his vices to the weaver of six shillings a week. The weaver of forty shillings had money instead of wit, the weaver of six shillings wit instead of money. During my experience of seventeen years within that factory the average earnings of first-rate hands, varying with the times, good and bad, were from six to nine shillings a week, second-rate workers from three to five shillings weekly. Some worked weeks,—months, for nothing.—How? Thus it was. If, from whatever cause except sickness, a girl was absent, she was marked down and fined to the extent and in proportion to the time of her absence. For example, if any female worker came to the gate after seven in the morning, she was not permitted to enter, lost the morning's work, and was fined a sixpence. A few of these rejected ones — it was almost a daily thing — would stroll about, unwilling to face a scolding at home. They went not there. Some would, and return to work when the gate opened at nine. The grave will ask, Could not they all have done so likewise? No, they, like yourselves, were some wise, and some weak. The question is an idle one, and worse than foolish, but you know you put it forth, and often. It were wiser work by far, and better, to clear away the stumbling blocks that beset the earlier paths of erring creatures rather than admire or grieve at the error. Give yourselves but the trouble to look for it, and you will find out a link or two precede crime. These *you* should cut. *You* may do it. The object chained, however willing, has seldom the power. These poor girls are loitering—idle, wandering between a laugh and a tear—the most slippery standing of any. Ten to one if that day, or the next two days find the fair truants at their looms. For each day absent there comes a fine of one shilling, hence three days absence required three days of hard working to clear scores with the "Company" for the follies of the week. This was not rare, but very common. Here was a Savings Bank truly inside out! Instead of wondering at the folly, rather ask how the fool subsisted in this work-for-nothing way? Where was her table spread? her fare what? and how looked her home? Condemn not, ye prosperous, ye untempted happy! Bless your dear selves. Your pantry full, and your feet warm. Saturday night creeps through yon dreary garret where her mother sits eagerly in fancy making "ends meet," balancing her little debts with her Jeanie's earnings! She knows not yet the truancy of yon morning—nor the fatal followings thereof—nor does she yet feel that the bread she devours is the price of her ruined lassie! There is a beginning, and if in her young and yet unhardened breast there speaks a portion of womanly regret—it is laughed away by her merry shop-mates. Her doom on earth is fixed.

Between three and four hundred male and female workers were promiscuously distributed over the work; the distinctive character of all sunk away. Man became less manly. Woman unlovely and rude. Many of these married, some pairs seemed happy, they were few and left the work whenever they could get webs and looms outside. Vacancies daily made, were daily filled—often by queer enough people, and from all parts, none too coarse for using. He who had never sought a better sight than an unwatched pocket — he, trained to the loom six months in Bridewell, came forth a journeyman weaver, and lo! his precious experiences were infused into the common moral puddle, and in due time did its work—became a fixture,—another pot of poison sunken in the common well, and drink they must. The poorest poor, the uneducated, the untrained poor, drank of it; yet the wise and well provided will often condemn, without one pitying look, nor *seek* to see that strong link between crime and cause!

The garden of Gordon's Hospital lay close by our work, and was at the time open to all during every day. There was quietness there, though encircled by noisy streets. There, of a summer day, we would meet—those of us who had a turn for reading—and gossip over all we knew of books and the outer world. Then came glimpses,—the only glimpses afforded us of true, and natural, and rational existence. Then would the shuttle rest for a time, and "a little time yet—a harder and a longer pull tomorrow will keep soul and body acquainted, and our utmost does no more." With such coaxing philosophy, and the warm sun and the green, aye green garden about us, what wonder if there was lost in that day's labour the cloth of a striped shirt? It was only a groat! The Wizard of Waverley had roused the world to wonders, and we wondered too. Byron was flinging around the terrible and beautiful of a distracted greatness. Moore was doing all he could for love-sick boys and girls,—yet they had never enough! Nearer and dearer to hearts like ours was the Ettrick Shepherd, then in his full tide of song and story; but nearer and dearer still than he, or any living songster—to us dearer—was our ill-fated fellow-craftsman, Tannahill, who had just then taken himself from a neglecting world, while yet that world waxed mellow in his lay. Poor weaver chiel! What we owe to thee! Your "Braes o' Balquidder," and "Yon Burnside," and "Gloomy Winter," and the "Minstrel's" wailing ditty, and the noble "Gleneiffer." Oh! how they did ring above the rattling of a hundred shuttles! Let me again proclaim the debt we owe those Song Spirits, as they walked in melody from loom to loom, ministering to the low-hearted; and when the breast was filled with everything but hope and happiness, and all but seared, let only break forth the healthy and vigorous chorus "A man's a man for a' that," the fagged weaver brightens up. His very shuttle skytes boldly along, and clatters through in faithful time to the tune of his merrier shopmates!

Who dare measure in doubt the restraining influences of these very Songs? To us they were all instead of sermons. Had one of us been bold enough to enter a church, he must have been ejected for the sake of decency. His forlorn and curiously patched habiliments would have contested the point of attraction with the ordinary eloquence of that period. So for all parties it was better that he kept to his garret, or wandered far "in the deep green wood." Church bells rang not for us. Poets were indeed our Priests. But for those, the last relic of our moral existence would have surely passed away!

Song was the dew drops that gathered during the long dark night of despondency, and were sure to glitter in the very first blink of the sun. Yonder you might have seen "Auld Robin Gray" wet the eyes that could be tearless amidst cold and hunger, and weariness, and pain. Surely, surely then there was to that heart one passage yet unclosed; and a way to carry something thither would save the dreary tenement. We had nothing to give but a kind look and a song. The soup-kitchen was open five months in two years. The dead were buried—now why will people always grumble? To us Virtue, in whatever shape, came only in shadow, but even by that we saw her sweet proportions, and sometimes fain would have sought a kind acquaintance with her. Thinking that the better features of humanity could not be utterly defaced where song and melody were permitted to exist, and that where they were not all crushed, Hope and Mercy might yet bless the spot, some waxed bold, and for a time took leave of those who were called to " sing ayont the moon," groping amidst the material around and stringing it up, ventured on a home-made lilt.—Short was the search to find a newly kindled love, or some old heart abreaking. Such was aye amongst us and not always unnoticed, nor, as ye shall see, unsung.

It was not enough that we merely chaunted, and listened; but some more ambitious, or idle if you will, they in time would try a self-conceived song. Just as if some funny little boy, bolder than the rest, would creep into the room where lay Neil Gow's fiddle, and touch a note or two he could not name. How proud he is! how blest! for he had made a sound, and more, his playmates heard it, faith! Here I will introduce one of these early touches, not for any merit of its own, but it will show that we could sometimes bear and even seek for our minds a short residence, though not elegant, at least sinless,—a fleeting visit of healthy things, though small they were in size and few in number. Spray from a gushing "linn," if it slackened not the thirst, it cooled the brow.

The following ditty had its foundation in one of those luckless doings which ever and aye follow misguided attachments; and in our abode of freedom these were almost the only kind of attachments known; so they were all on the wrong side of durability or happiness.

AIR—"*Lass, gin you lo'e me, tell me noo.*"

We'll meet in yon wood, 'neath a starless sky,
  When wrestling leaves forsake ilk tree;
We mauna speak mair o' the days gane by,
  Nor o' friends that again we *never* maun see:
  Nae weak word o' mine shall remembrance gie
  O' vows that were made and were broken to me:
I'll seem in my silence to reckon them dead,
A' wither'd and lost as the leaves that we tread.

Alane ye maun meet me, when midnight is near,
  By yon blighted auld bush that we fatally ken;
The voice that allured me, O! let me nae hear,
  For my heart mauna beat to its music again.
  In darkness we'll meet, and in silence remain;
  Ilk word now and look now, were mockful or vain;
Ae mute moment mourn the dream that misled,
Syne sinder as cauld as the leaves that we tread.

This ditty was sung in the weaving shops, and when in the warbling of one who could lend a good voice to the occasion, and could coax the words and air into a sort of social understanding, then was it a song.

I cannot remember the precise date of this melancholy creation. Sure enough some time about

Ae, *one*
Auld, *old*
Gie, *give*
Gin, *if*
Ilk, *every*
Ken, *know*
Mair, *more*
Mauna, *must not*
Maun, *may*
Nae, *no*
Noo, *now*
Sinder, *separate*
Syne, *then*

1826, when banks were falling like meteors, but rather oftener; the world seemed hurrying to ruin. The very Sun on high lent a helping heat—kindling Mirrimachi. Cauld Caledonia lay baked and cracked—yielding Lilliputian crops—a parody on corn. Amidst all this, and more than all this, weavers would sing. The factory-distinguished writer of these verses, though at first indifferent, yet as they became more favoured by his shopmates, and had actually been named without the gates, conceit gradually stole away his better judgment; and at last one of his eyes—the weather eye—became firmly shut, while the other was immoveably fixed on Parnassus. Why should *his* powers live and die in this black boundary? His song not be heard beyond the unpoetical brick walls of a factory? It was settled. He is off. The shuttle for a time may go rot. No heed, no care of the hungry hours and hard weaving that must follow. There he goes, and over his beating heart lies a well-folded, fairly-copied version of his first-born, as he wends his way to the printing-office of the *Aberdeen Journal.*

One special crony, and only one, was in confidence, and no mean sharer was he in the unutterably curious feeling that sets in on the first throes of authorship. Early on the morning of publication the anxious pair stood watchfully in a court that led to the printing-office. The *Confidant* was in that moderately troublesome state known as fidgets, with now and then a qualm, inasmuch as having talked away two days' work, there was not withal to settle up matters in his boarding-house that night. The *Principal*, although in the very same plight, felt not the very same way. His pain—for pain it was—had no connection with aught on earth, save and except the printing-office on which he gazed. Did his verses exist in *print?*

Woes on me! Why don't they buy a paper? Man after man, lad and elderly woman, passed each other with Journal at nose, heedless of all beside.

"Ask that man for a peep."

"Have not I besought it of twenty?"

"Then let us try that chappie coming up."

This was meant for a sulky little fellow, who refused flat to open his paper. Patience could do no more; it *becked** away, quite; good manners and honesty followed. We were "left to ourselves." The obstinate journal bearer was borne into a house entry; we shut the door; and while he kicked and roared, we groped for the Poor Man's Corner in the Journal, and were blest — the song was there!

* * * * *

Weaving, as year after year it dwindled, became at length an evendown waste of life—a mere permission to breathe. Sickened at the very sameness

* Bowed.

in this mode of dying, I resolved to vary the method, and taste, by way of change, Sorrow further South. I found her grim Ladyship at last; but not until I had enjoyed nine years of such happiness as seldom visits man.

In the spring of 1837,* the failure of certain great commercial establishments in America, combining with other causes, silenced, in one week, upwards of six thousand looms in Dundee, and the various agencies in its connexion, and spread dismay throughout the whole county of Forfar. Amongst the many villages thus trade-stricken, none felt the blow more severely than that of Newtyle, near Cupar-Angus. This village was new, having sprung up since the completion of the Dundee Railway, a few years before. It consisted chiefly of weaving-shops and dwellings for the weavers. The inhabitants, about two hundred in number, were strangers to the place and to each other, having been recently collected from distant places by advertisements promising them many advantages, but which, when the evil day came, were little regarded. While employers were, some unwilling and many unable, to do any-

* While in London (1841), I was introduced to Mr. Robert Chambers, of the *Edinburgh Journal*. In course of gossip, I related to him what led to the production of an " Ode to my Flute." He liked the story, and, at his request, I wrote it.

thing for the relief of those whom they had brought together for their own purposes, the people of the neighbourhood, including those of the old village of Newtyle, regarded them with stern prejudice, as intruders "that naebody kent naething aboot." It were too much to say that they were positively persecuted by their neighbours, but certainly they received no sympathy in their distresses from that quarter, much less any relief.

A little while thinned the village, those only remaining who had many children, and were obliged to consider well before they started. To these (and I was of the number) one web was supplied weekly, bringing five shillings. The weaver will know what sort of job the weaving of an "Osnaburg" was at that price. It had been a stiff winter and unkindly spring, but it passed away, as other winters and springs must do. I will not expatiate on six human lives subsisting on five shillings weekly—on babies prematurely thoughtful—on comely faces withering—on desponding youth, and too quickly declining age. These things are perhaps too often *talked of*. Let me describe but one morning of modified starvation at Newtyle, and then pass on.

Imagine a cold spring forenoon. It is eleven o'clock, but our little dwelling shows none of the signs of that time of day. The four children are still asleep. There is a bed-cover hung before the window, to keep all within as much like night as possible; and the mother sits beside the beds of her children, to lull them back to sleep whenever any shows an inclination to awake. For this there is a cause, for our weekly five shillings have not come as expected, and the only food in the house consists of a handful of oatmeal saved from the supper of last night. Our fuel is also exhausted. My wife and I were conversing in sunken whispers about making an attempt to cook the handful of meal, when the youngest child awoke beyond its mother's power to hush it again to sleep, and then fell a whimpering, and finally broke out in a steady scream, rendering it impossible any longer to keep the rest in a state of unconsciousness. Face after face sprang up, each with one consent exclaiming, "Oh, mither, mither, gie me a piece!" How weak a word is sorrow to apply to the feelings of myself and wife during the remainder of that dreary forenoon!

We thus lingered on during the spring, still hoping that things would come a little round, or that at least warmer weather would enable us, with more safety, to venture on a change of residence. At length, seeing that our strength was rapidly declining, I resolved to wait no longer. Proceeding to Dundee, I there exchanged at a pawnbroker's, a last and most valued relic of better days, for ten shillings, four of which I spent on such little articles as usually constitute "a pack," designing this to be carried by my wife, while other four shillings I expended on second-hand books, as a stock of merchandize for myself; but I was very unfortunate in my selection, which consisted chiefly of little volumes, containing abridgements of modern authors, these authors being little to the general taste of a rustic population.

On a Thursday morning we forsook our melancholy habitation, leaving in it my two looms and some furniture (for we thought of returning to it), and the key with the landlord. On the third day, Saturday, we passed through the village of Inchture, in the Carse of Gowrie, and proceeded towards Kinnaird. Sunset was followed by cold sour east winds and rain. The children becoming weary and fretful, we made frequent inquiries of other forlorn looking beings whom we met, to ascertain which farm-town in the vicinity was most likely to afford us quarters. Jean was sorely exhausted, bearing an infant constantly at her breast, and often carrying the youngest boy also, who had fairly broken down in the course of the day. It was nine o'clock when we approached the large and comfortable-looking steading of Balguay, standing about a quarter of a mile off the road. Leaving my poor flock on the wayside, I pushed down the path to the farm-house with considerable confidence, for I had been informed that Balguay (meaning, by this local appellation, the farmer) was a humane man, who never turned the wanderer from his door. Unfortunately for us, the worthy farmer, (Playfair,) was from home, and not expected to return that night. His housekeeper had admitted several poor people already, and could admit no more. I pleaded with her the infancy of my family, the lateness of the night, and their utter unfitness to proceed—that we sought nothing but shelter——that the meanest shed would be a blessing. Heaven's mercy was never more earnestly pleaded for than was a night's lodging by me on that occasion; but "No, no, no," was the unvarying answer to all my entreaties.

I returned to my family; they had crept closer together, and all, except the mother, were fast asleep.

"Oh, Willie, Willie! what keepit ye?" inquired the trembling woman. "I'm dootfu' o' Jeanie," she added; "isna she waesome like? Let's in frae the cauld."

"We've nae way to gang, lass," said I, "whate'er come o' us. Yon folk winna hae us."

Few more words passed. I drew her mantle over the wet and chilled sleepers, and sat down beside them. My head throbbed with pain, and for a time became the tenement of thoughts I would not now reveal. They partook less of sorrow than of indignation, and it seemed to me that this same world was a thing very much to be hated; and, on the whole, the sooner that one like me could get out of it, the better for its sake and my own. I felt myself, as it were, shut out from mankind—enclosed—prisoned in misery—no outlook—none! My miserable wife and little ones, who alone cared for me—what would I not have done for their sakes at that hour! Here let me speak out—and be heard, too, while I tell it—that the world does not at all times know how unsafely it sits—when Despair has loosed Honour's last hold upon the heart—when transcendent Wretchedness lays weeping Reason in the dust—when every unsympathizing onlooker is deemed an enemy—who THEN can limit the consequences? For my own part, I confess that, ever since that dreadful night, I can never hear of an extraordinary criminal, without the wish to pierce through the mere judicial view of his career, under which, I am persuaded, there would often be found to exist an unseen impulse — a chain, with one end fixed in Nature's holiest ground, that drew him on to his destiny.

The gloamin' light was scarcely sufficient to allow me to write a note, which I carried to a stately mansion hard by.* It was to entreat what we had been denied at Balguay. This application was also fruitless. The servant had been ordered to take in no such notes, and he could not break through the rule. On rejoining my little group, my heart lightened at the presence of a serving-man, who at that moment came near, and who, observing our wretchedness, could not pass without endeavouring to succour us. The kind

* Inchmartine; but not at that time occupied by its proprietor Mr. Allen, who was then, and is still, a minor.

words of this *worthy peasant** sunk deep into our hearts. I do not know his name; but never can I forget him. Assisted by him, we arrived, about eleven o'clock, at the farm-house of John Cooper, West-town of Kinnaird, where we were immediately admitted. The accommodation, we were told, was poor; but what an alternative from the storm-beaten wayside! The servants were not yet in bed; and we were permitted a short time to warm ourselves at the bothy fire. During this interval, the infant seemed to revive; it fastened heartily to the breast, and soon fell asleep. We were next led to an out-house. A man stood by with a lantern, while, with straw and blankets, we made a pretty fair bed. In less than half an hour, the whole slept sweetly in their dark and almost roofless dormitory.

I think it must have been between three and four o'clock when Jean wakened me. Oh, that scream!—I think I can hear it now. The other children, startled from sleep, joined in frightful wail over their *dead sister*. Our poor Jeanie had, unobserved by us, sunk during the night under the effects of the exposure of the preceding evening, following, as it did, a long course of hardship, too great to be borne by a young frame. Such a visitation could only be sustained by one hardened to misery and

---

* Knockespock, and I have written twice to Mr. Cooper, to know his name, but never received an answer.

wearied of existence. I sat a while and looked on them; comfort I had none to give—none to take; I spake not—what could be said—words? Oh, no! the worst is over when words can serve us. And yet it is not just when the wound is given that pain is felt. How comes it, I wonder, that minor evils will affect even to agony, while paramount sorrow overdoes itself, and stands in stultified calmness? Strange to say, on first becoming aware of the bereavement of that terrible night, I sat for some minutes gazing upwards at the fluttering and wheeling movements of a party of swallows, our fellow-lodgers, which had been disturbed by our unearthly outcry.

After a while, I proceeded to awaken the people in the house, who entered at once into our feelings, and did every thing which Christian kindness could dictate as proper to be done on the occasion. A numerous and respectable party of neighbours assembled that day to assist at the funeral. In an obscure corner of Kinnaird kirkyard lies our favourite, little Jeanie.

Early on Monday, we resumed our heartless pilgrimage—wandering onwards, without any settled purpose or end. The busy, singing world above us was a nuisance; and around, the loaded fields bore nothing for us—we were things apart. Nor knew we where that night our couch might be, or where, to-morrow, our grave. 'Tis but fair to say, however, that our children never were ill-off during the day-time. Where our goods were not bought, we were, nevertheless, offered "a piece to the bairnies." One thing which might contribute to this was, that our appearance, as yet, was respectable, and it seemed as if the people saw in us neither the shrewd hawker nor the habitual mendicant, so that we were better supplied with food than had been our lot for many a month before.

But oh, the ever-recurring sunset! Then came the hour of sad conjecturing and sorrowful outlook. To seek lodging at a farm before sunset, was to insure refusal. After nightfall, the children, worn out with the day's wanderings, turned fretful, and slept whenever we sat down. After experience taught us cunning in this, as in other things—the tactics of habitual vagrants being to remain in concealment near a farm of good name, until a suitable lateness warranted the attack. This night, however, we felt so much in need of a comfortable resting-place, that it was agreed we should make for Errol. There we settled for the night at a house kept for the humblest description of "travellers." It is one of those places of entertainment whose most engaging feature is the easy price. Its inmates, unaccustomed even to the luxury of a fire, easily enough dispense with seats; and where five or six people are packed up alive in one box, a superabundance of bed-clothes would be found uncomfortable. Hence the easy charges. Our fellow-lodgers were of all nations, to the amount of two dozen or so.

As it has been my lot, since then, to pass many a night and day in similar society, and, having somewhat of a turn for observation, my memory could furnish many records of " gangrel bodies," that are not altogether wanting in interest; but of that another time. One case, however, has, in some points, so much of resemblance to my own, at one period, that I would fain notice it here. At the gloamin' hour, we entered the village of Errol in the Carse of Gowrie. In the main street, a group of people had gathered round a man, and stood silent and attentive, as if expecting some display or another. I wondered, for a moment, whether the man was a preacher, and at a dead stop for material. The grave and benevolent expression on his comely face, as well as the dark hue of his apparel, misled me so far; and for the rest, the bewilderment of his look certainly intimated that, whatever the employment, his lips had " closed for the season." It was not so. I knew it all afterwards. He had been just then singing—for the first time, singing in the streets. I heard his song. Surely, surely, thought I, it comes from his very heart; such earnestness, such sorrowful sweetness! Misery makes niggards of us, and at times sympathies will actually become self-consumed; yet the man and his " Light of other days," haunted my fancy, even to my motley lodgings—my caravansarie—my bield of meal-bags and monsters. Here, aside from the coarse and bloated inmates of our dwelling, a respectable-looking woman sat nursing a sick infant—a poor, withered, corpse-like baby, with little of life there but the wailing, wailing, that would not be stilled. One or two of our neighbours seemed to sympathize with the young and lonely mother; others grumbled harshly to want their sleep. By-and-by, another lodger entered. It was the man—the very singing-man—I heard in the gloamin'. In a moment he was in our group, leaning over his dying infant! Now, just think of singing, and *that* the key-note: I will not bother you with remarks.

"I have wearied sadly for your coming, James," said the woman.

"It's so dark out bye the nicht," he replied, "I only faund out this door by our wean greetin'."

Many a time, since that sad night, have I seen him and his interesting family snug and happy at their own hearth. A feeling unknown to the many, sprung up between us—it endures for life—like that of creatures who had met in a desert. Fain would I at this moment introduce his story, for it is a sad one—his name, his sufferings, and his amiabilities. But no; there are minds anew in the world little enough, cruel enough, to remind him, as they have me, of the desolate day that was never chosen; and envy sufficient to blot his prosperity—to find invidious causes for his calamity—for sorrows and circumstances that no man would seek. With minds like these, to be once down is never to look up again—once humbled, nothing after is sufficiently low. His infant died ere he left that lodging-house. In justice to silent sufferers, as well as to the unwary benevolent, it is well to mention here a cast of imposture carried on by the thoroughbred, never-give-up, "all right" class of beggarhood. In common tramp-houses, wherein this class mostly harbour, a death is, in a double sense, a godsend—such, indeed, is to them a gracious notice, even when it comes in a "*fair strae*"* kind of way. But if the decease has aught about it of the extraordinary, so as to attract local sympathy, out of that comes a true Christmas. Every crutch is on end—every bag hoisted—every face stretched to the nonce, and these things spread to every point, each wailing the loss of child, mother, brother, sister, or wife—or all together, rather than not melt. This and shipwrecks form a kind of staple in the commonwealth of *Gaberlunzie*.

Leaving Errol next day, we passed up the Carse to Perth, were kept there a few days by some old acquaintances, started from thence towards Methven, sold little on the way thither, but were kindly treated by the workers at Huntingtower and Cromwell Park. The people there were themselves on limited work—indeed, many of them had none; yet they shared their little substance with those that

---

* Not by foul means.

had less. It is always so; but for the poor, the poorer would perish.

Just before entering Methven, I sold a small book to a person breaking stones for the road. After some conversation, I discovered he was musical, and was strongly tempted to sell him my flute. He had taken a fancy to it, and offered a good price. I resisted; it had long been my companion, and sometimes my solace; and indeed, to speak truth, I had, for some days past, attended to certain "forlorn hope" whisperings, implying the possible necessity of using that instrument in a way more to be lamented than admired. The sum total of my earthly moneys was fivepence-halfpenny, which my little volume had seduced from the pocket of the musical lapidary. With this treasure, we sat by the fireside of Mrs. L.'s lodging-house in Methven. The good woman gave us to understand that our entertainment would cost sixpence, at the same time declaring it to be a standing rule in her establishment to see payment made of all such matters before the parties "took aff their shoon." I only wondered, when I looked round on the bare feet that luxuriated about her hearth, how she contrived to put this test into execution. The demand for our lodging-money was decided, and so was I. I took my woe-worn partner aside, whispered her to pick my flute from out our "budgets," put on her mantle, and follow me. As we went along, I disclosed my purpose of playing in the outskirts of the village. This was a new line of action, not to be taken without some qualms. But then the landlady! Besides, nobler natures, and higher names than I could ever aim at, had betaken themselves to similar means. Homer had sung his epics for a morsel of bread; Goldsmith had piped his way over half the Continent. These were precedents indeed! Moreover, neither of these worthies had children in Methven or elsewhere, that ever I heard of. Nor is it recorded in the history of those great men, whether they had at any time been under the compulsion of a landlady who attached a special consequence to the moment that undid the shoe-tie.

Musing over these and many other considerations, we found ourselves in a beautiful green lane, fairly out of the town, and opposite a genteel-looking house, at the windows of which sat several well-dressed people. I think that it might be our bewildered and hesitating movements that attracted their notice—perhaps not favourably.

"A quarter of an hour longer," said I, "and it will be darker; let us walk out a bit."

The sun had been down a good while, and the gloamin' was lovely. In spite of everything, I felt a momentary reprieve. I dipped my dry flute in a little burn, and began to play. It rang sweetly amongst the trees. I moved on and on, still playing, and still *facing* the town. "The flowers of the forest" brought me before the house lately mentioned. My music raised one window after another, and in less than ten minutes put me in possession of 3s. 9d. of good British money. I sent the mother home with this treasure, and directed her to send our little girl to me. It was by this time nearly dark. Every one says, " Things just need a beginning." I have had a beginning, and a very good one too. I had also a turn for strathspeys, and there appeared to be a run upon them. By this time I was nearing the middle of the town. When I finally made my way, and retired to my lodging, it was with five shillings and some pence, in addition to what was given us. My little girl got a beautiful shawl, and some articles of wearing apparel.

Shall I not bless the good folk of Methven? Let me ever chance to meet a Methven weaver in distress, and I will share my last bannock with him. These men—for I knew them, as they knew me, by instinct—these men not only helped me themselves, but testified their gratitude to every one that did so. There was enough to encourage further perseverance; but I felt, after all, that I had begun too late in life ever to acquire that "ease and grace" indispensable to him who would successfully " *carry the gaberlunzie on.*" I felt I must forego it, at least in a downright street capacity.

After some consideration, another mode of exercising my talents for support occurred to me. I had, ever since I remember, an irrepressible tendency to make verses, and many of these had won applause from my friends and fellow-workmen, so I determined to press this faculty into my service on the present occasion. Accordingly, after sundry down-sittings and contemplations, by waysides and in barns, my Muse produced the following ode

TO MY FLUTE.

It's nae to harp, to lyre, nor lute,
   I ettle now to sing;
To thee alane, my lo'esome flute,
   This hamely strain I bring!
Oh! let us flee on memory's wing,
   O'er twice ten winters flee,
An' try ance mair that ae sweet spring
   Whilk young love breathed in thee.

Companion o' my happy *then*,
   Wi' smilin' frien's around;
In ilka but, in ilka ben,*
   A couthie, welcome found—
Ere yet thy master proved the wound
   That ne'er gaed scaithless by;
That gi'es to flutes their saftest sound,
   To hearts their saddest sigh.

Since then, my bairns hae danced to thee,
   To thee my Jean has sung;
And monie a nicht, wi' guiltless glee,
   Our hearty hallan rung.

Bairns, *children.*   Hallan, *roof tree.*   Lo'esome, *beloved.*
Couthie, *kindly.*   Ilka, *every.*   Spring, *tune.*
Ettle, *attempt.*

* The but is the parlour, the ben the kitchen end of every Scotch home.

But noo, wi' hardship worn and stung,
  I'll roam the warld about;
For her and for our friendless young,
  Come forth, my faithful flute!

Your artless notes may win the ear
  That wadna hear me speak;
And for your sake that pity spare,
  My full heart couldna seek.
And whan the winter's cranreuch bleak
  Drives houseless bodies in,
We'll ablins get the ingle-cheek,
  A' for your lichtsome din.

This I designed to be printed on fine paper, with a fly-leaf attached, and folded in the style of a note, to be presented to none *under* a footman, by a decently-dressed, modest-looking man (myself, of course), who, after waiting ten minutes, the time wanted to utter the "Oh, la's!" and "Who may he be's?" would, I expected, be asked into the drawing-room, where the admiring circle should be ravished with his sweet-toned minstrelsy. After compliments sufficient for any mere man, this person I supposed to retire with that in his pocket that could not rightly be expended without a great deal of prudent consideration. Such was my dream. I accordingly proceeded to act as I had designed. With a few copies of my poem, I set out once more upon my travels, and, to do justice to the scheme, it

Aiblins, *perhaps*.   Ingle cheek, *chimney corner*.   Lichtsome, *merry noise*.
Cranreuch, *piercing wind*.

was, on several occasions, successful to the extent anticipated. In one laird's house I received a guerdon of half a guinea; but, after all, it was but beggar's work, and my soul in time grew sick of it. It was with no sighings after flesh-pots that, in a few weeks, on times becoming a little better, I settled down once more to my loom.

Weaving about a year in Aberdeen, I accidentally obtained a job from a customary* weaver in the Garioch, a district bordering on Mar and Strathbogie, in Aberdeenshire. This proving far more profitable than factory work, induced me to remove my family from Aberdeen to Inverury, a place centrical and convenient to the call of employers in the customary line. Nine months after our settlement here, she died—Jean—the mother of my family—partner of my wanderings—the unmurmuring sharer in all my difficulties, left us—left us, too, just as the last cold cloud was passing, ere the outbreak of a brighter day. That cloud passed, but the warmth that followed lost half its value to me, she being no partaker therein.

In January, 1841, precisely one year after having taken residence at Inverury, my better star had, all unknown to me, determined to take a turn on the upward way. Customary work almost ceases here at this season, and remains dull for several months. I had been unemployed thus for two weeks. To

* Household.

lull the weariness, and make away with very tedious hours, I composed small poems on subjects that pleased me. This I did, without a glance beyond the selfish pleasure one finds in shaping out a fixed and tangible abode to feelings and fancies dear to the memory. One of these compositions I sent to the *Aberdeen Herald*, and three weeks after it appeared anonymously in that paper, ushered by a notice of sympathy from the editor, Mr. Adam, to whom I was then entirely unknown. This poem, No. 1 of *The Blind Boy's Pranks*, was copied into most newspapers in the kingdom. With a rather full average of human vanity in my disposition, all this, at another time, would have been pleasing enough; but as it was, the first gleam of public favour had not power to withdraw my mind from what was before me, nor to brighten the dreary outlook.

On a cold, cold winter day of February, we sat alone, my little ones and I, looking on the last meal procurable by honourable means. My purpose was settled—our wearables, such as they were, lay packed up for the journey—Aberdeen and the House of Refuge our next home. I felt resigned. True, we might have breathed on a little while longer, had I been able to worm through all the creeping intricacies that lie between starvation and parish charities. But, oh! how preferable, surely, the unseen, silent sadness in a House of Refuge to the thousand and one heartless queries, taunts, and grumblings, that accompany the Elder's " eighteenpence." Heaven averted all these, at any rate. On the forenoon of that same day, there came a post letter, dated *Aberdeen Journal Office*. The nature of that letter will be sufficiently understood by the following extract from that paper :—

" The beautiful verses entitled *The Blind Boy's Pranks*, the production of a " Serf,"* which appeared in our paper of the 20th January [copied from the *Herald*, where it *first* appeared], are, we doubt not, fresh in the memory of many of our readers. It will delight them to learn that the humble yet gifted author has not passed unnoticed or unrewarded. We have had the pleasure of conveying to him, from a gentleman of this county, (the friend of native genius,) a very substantial token of his admiration; and make no apology for submitting to our readers the simple tale of thanks with which it has been received. The genuine spirit of poetry pervades *The Blind Boy's Pranks;* and is no less conspicuous in the lines which follow. They cannot fail to create an interest in the *welfare of the hard-working and talented* " Serf:"—

" Inverury, Feb. 7, 1841.

" DEAR SIR,—I have this hour received your kind letter, enclosing another, with five pounds, from Knockespock. Unaccustomed—utterly unaccustomed as I have been to such correspondents,

* The signature originally appended to the verses.

and with such accompaniments, what shall I say? Nothing now—indeed, I cannot; neither can I delay this acknowledgment—but after hours will speak my gratitude. That gentleman shall hear from me soon. Meantime, I subjoin a little thing* that happened to be in the '*loom*' when yours came to hand. You are fairly entitled to the freshest of my homely productions. Through your hand, for the first time in my life, has my rhyming brought me aught beyond 'fusionless' praise—indeed, beyond that, I have never hoped nor wished; but now that, through the munificence of Knockespock, my physical struggle is slackened, I foresee that my pursuits (mentally) may be less fettered and have a wider range. Oh! sir, it is difficult for those in other circumstances to think what a strife is his who has to battle lip-deep in poverty, with a motherless family and a *poetical temperament!* The last item the worst—inasmuch as it enhances tenfold the pain that is *frequent*, and the joy that is *rare*. Let sincerity atone for the want of elegance in, "Dear Sir,

"Your grateful and obliged

" W. Thom."

" To D. Chalmers, Esq,, Aberdeen,
  Editor of the *Journal*."

I wrote my thanks to Knockespock, as follows:—

* " Oh, Mary! when ye think of me."

WILLIAM THOM TO K.

"Inverury, March 30th, 1841.

"HONOURED SIR,—I fear that I have too long delayed the performance of a duty, which, though not acted, has never for an hour forsaken my thoughts. Had I been schooled in the language of thanksgiving I would ere now have directly acknowledged my gratitude, but I knew not how to express the fulness of my heart, and at the same time spare the delicacy of my benefactor. It was just last night I thought, after all, the plain way was the best—so I will tell you how matters stood, and how they stand, and leave you to shape out conclusions.

"That day your letter reached me, I and my family had looked on the last *meal procurable by honourable means*. I had not only resolved, but was actually 'packing up' for Aberdeen, and the House of Refuge—for you will know that I had not been in this parish* long enough to entitle me to its assistance. Indeed, had it been otherwise, I should have preferred the unseen sadness of the 'House' to the thousand and one heartless queries of the beadle. There were yet eight or ten weeks to pass ere the season of 'Customary' Weaving (to which

---

* It requires an industrial residence of three years in Scotland before persons become chargeable.

alone I was bred) could commence. I might have *breathed* through that space by supplication, etc., but the Lord averted—and when your kindness was known it was universally admitted to be a ' Heaven-inspired act.' Had you beheld the wild glee of my boys! had you seen the tears of their pretty sister that day! Oh! sir, to a kind heart *there* was praise indeed, sweeter than sycophant e'er uttered, or poet sung! Well, well, from that hour to this we have never known want. The fuss that followed No. 1 of *The Pranks,* in connection with Knockespock's notice, at once flattered my self-love and filled my '*cog.*'* Cheerfully do I now push on—a little bit of weaving, not so bitterly adhered to, as has been, and now and then a *job musical*, for you must know my celebrity divides between poet and flute-player—and being attached to a local band, we occasionally get employed in these districts. There is a good deal of my time spent in the adjustment of my womanless household, my lassie being yet only *ten*—but I snatch every disposable hour, and am industrious towards the creation of my book, which I think may be in its calf-skin jacket by the end of harvest. Will you, my dear sir, accept the dedication? Oh do not deny me that bright opportunity to at once tell the world my gratitude, and to *whose* timely interference is due the existence of my simple lays. A thousand to one if ever

---

* A dish.

No. 2 of *The Blind Boy* would have *seen* the light, but for the good fortune of its predecessor.

"I am, honoured Sir,
"All *you* would wish a poor man to be,
"Your servant,
"WILLIAM THOM."

Soon after Mr. Gordon sent a letter containing many inquiries concerning my situation and prospects. My reply may be acceptable at this point of the story, as it embodies the *pith* of his letter, and exhibits that kind of family statistics which his amiable nature seeks out, in every instance to help and to heal. It would fill a volume what I have witnessed of that gentleman's benevolent doings, and of the delight he enjoys in the happiness of a fellow-creature; but let me speak now only of the instance at hand. After chastising myself for not attending more promptly to his very first communication, my reply to his second runs thus:—

"As to the long silence that ensued, I must recur to my former plea—namely, my inability to express my own feelings, with a certainty all the while, that I did not trespass on those of my benefactor. Again I sincerely ask pardon; and let this farther consideration plead for me, that my lowly breeding has hid from me those nice and proper distinctions recognised by people of education and superior training—even *now*, I know not, thus speaking, how far I may commit myself, and I beg leave to proceed to the queries as they stand in your letter, replying to all in single-hearted sincerity.

"'*What was you bred to?*' Born in Aberdeen, the son of a widow unable to keep me at home idle, I was, when ten years of age, placed in a public factory, where I served an apprenticeship of four years, at the end of which I entered another great weaving establishment, 'Gordon, Barron, and Co.,' where I continued seventeen years. During my apprenticeship I had picked up a little reading and writing. Afterwards set about studying Latin—went so far, but was fairly defeated through want of time, &c.—having the while to support my mother, who was getting frail. However, I continued to gather something of arithmetic and music, both of which I have mastered so far as to render further progress easy did I see it requisite. I play the German flute tolerably in general subjects, but in my native melodies, lively or pathetic, to *few* will I lay it down. I have every Scotch song that is worth singing; and though my vocal capability is somewhat limited, I can convey a pretty fair idea of what a Scotch song *ought* to be.

"So much for '*acquirements.*' You next ask my '*age and state of health?*' I am *forty-two*—my health not robust but evenly; a lameness of one leg, occasioned by my being, when in infancy, crushed under the wheel of a carriage. This unfits me for work requiring extra personal strength; and indeed it is mostly owing to little mechanical appliances of my own contriving, that I am enabled to subject the more laborious parts of my calling to the limits of my very stinted bodily power.

" '*The number and age of my family?*' Three—Elizabeth, aged ten and a half years, William eight, and James five.

" My wife died in childbed, last November; my girl does the best she can by way of housekeeper; the boys are at school. I cannot spare the lassie, so she gets a lesson at home.

" '*Description of my dwelling.*'—I occupy two trim little garrets in a house belonging to Sir Robert Elphinstone, lately built on the market stance of Inverury. We have everything required in our humble way; perhaps our blankets pressed a little too lightly during the late severe winter, but then we crept closer together—that is gone—'tis summer now, and we are hopeful that next winter will bring better things.

" '*Means of Living*' — employed seven or eight months yearly in customary weaving—that is, a country weaver who wants a journeyman sends for me. I assist in making bedding, shirting, and other household stuffs. When his customers are served, I am discharged, and so ends the *season*. During that time I earn from ten to twelve shillings a week; pay the master generally four shillings for my 'keep,' and remit the rest to my family. In this way, we moved on happy enough. Ambition, or something like it, would now and then whisper me into discontent. But now, how blest would I deem myself had I my beloved partner again, and the same difficulties to retrace. I eke out the blank portions of the season by going into a factory. Here the young and vigorous only can exceed six shillings weekly. This alone is my period of privation; however, it is wonderful how nicely we get on. A little job now and then, in the musical way, puts all right again. I don't drink, as little at any rate as possible. I have been vain enough to set some value on my mind, and it being all that I possess now, and the only thing likely to put me in possession of aught afterwards, I would not willingly *drown* it.

"'*My Books*'—I have few of my own—pick up a loan where it can be had: so of course my reading is without choice or system. Your question with regard to '*Religion*'—I believe in God, and in Christ the Saviour of mankind.—'*What do I look forward to in life?*' Lately I looked to nothing but increasing labour and decreasing strength—interminable toil and ultimate starvation—such is the fate of nine-tenths of my brethren—but now daylight breaks on my destiny. Since you wrote me, my verses have attracted the notice of several literary gentlemen in Edinburgh, who have tendered friendship to me, and are to use their influence in my behalf in the event of my publishing. Mr. M., of the *Weekly Chronicle*, has frequently mentioned me in kindness.* Hence I dream of making my 'escape' from the loom; and of being enabled to pull my little ones out from amongst 'folk's feet.' I fully appreciate your friendly counsel regarding premature publication, and shall attend to it; also to the selection of subjects, but I would not be diverted from my original purpose anent the dedication to you. God knows, I have been taught the value of a shilling, but have never yet stooped to an unbecoming action to obtain one; and although they were in my neighbourhood (as I don't know if they are) that would better me †—yet, sir, permit me to abide by my first notion.

"I had nearly forgot that you ask me whether I possess '*Good common sense as well as poetical ability?*' Well, really, sir, I cannot say: most people erect their own standard in that matter, and gene-

---

* Literature, when pursued as a profession, confers dignity on its votary; but when, as in the case of the amiable and gifted Thom of Inverury, Aberdeenshire, and many others of his class similarly situated, it is resorted to amid the little relaxation which a laborious profession allows, we confess we reverence that man who can thus vindicate the superiority of mind over matter. Many are content to eat, to sleep, and do a little work again; the day-spring conveys to such minds no other feeling than that they must rise and work; and the evening closes around them and glads their dull faculties with only the visions of a supper and a bed. This is the animal, the vegetable life which but too many live, to the utter abasement of intellect and elevated feeling."—*Edinburgh Weekly Chronicle*, Feb. 1841.

† Knockespock had suggested to me that there might be others to whom I might dedicate more advantageously than to him.

rally award to themselves a pretty fair share; and few are found grumbling with the distribution. I have looked as closely as my degree permitted, upon man, his ways and his wishes, and I have tasted in my own experience some of life's bitterest tastings; hence I have obtained some shrewd glimpses of what calls common sense into action, and what follows the action wherein common sense has no share.

"You speak of '*respectable references:*' Dr. Thomson here has known me these two years, being the amount of my residence in this place; Mr. M'Naughtan, manager to Gordon, Barron, & Co., Aberdeen. To these I can refer, and if they do not call me a good, I dare them to call me a bad man. By the way, I have never sought to cultivate an acquaintance amongst those not in my immediate degree, and am little known: my hands recommended me to my employers, and beyond that I seldom thought.* I am, &c., &c.,

"WILLIAM THOM."

I received another note from Knockespock, the tenor of which may be best gathered from my reply which follows.

---

* Let it be remembered that these questions were put to the *Poet*, from no idle curiosity or intolerance, but to ascertain if the situation of a Schoolmaster would suit him.

J. A. G.

"Aberdeen, April 29, 1841.

"HONOURED SIR,—Your letter, with its enclosure, reached me on the 27th. I immediately set about the arrangements pointed out to me, so my lassie and I are thus far on the way to London, very much delighted with every thing and every body, the world and all therein lovelier than before, just because *we* are happy,—" thereby hangs a tale." I could philosophize, and speak of the unseen sympathies that exist between the breeches pocket and Nature's " lovely green." Well, we left our little kinsfolks, Will and Jamie, very ill at heart, and I thought never to have got Betsy and William parted: indeed, sir, I once thought of fetching him along. I am content to know that they will be well looked to. I procured a careful and decent female to keep house, and laid in sufficiency for two months' comfort. There is something in your doings in regard of me that has struck every body in this quarter. There is in it so much of what might be termed the *romance of reality*. Do you remember how matters stood with me when I got your first letter? Well, I was, when this one came, on my way to *Pitmachie* to resume my toils of the "*season;*" aye, sir, and very VERY thankful indeed for the " chance of getting employment." I cannot "prepare" to write, therefore it is to be hoped you will excuse my " off-loof" way.

"Your most obedient and humble servant,

"W. THOM."

Ten days after, I and little Betsy were *dashing* along in a handsome carriage through the streets of London. Here was a change sufficient to turn the head of a bewildered weaver. Under the roof of my kind friends Mr. and Mrs. Gordon, I remained upwards of four months, and paid great attention to all I saw and heard. I was introduced to many of the master minds of yon great city. In the studio of Sir Francis Chantrey, I conversed with the lamented Allan Cunningham. I have listened to the eloquence, and heard the nonsense of those who give laws to the people. I saw Majesty and Misery, and many of the paths between. Many a pleasure was put within my power; and many are the delights of happy England, and kind the hearts therein; yet I longed for Scotland, and am again upon my heather, and at my loom. Alas! for the loom, though! Hitherto it has been to me the ship on which I voyaged o'er life—Happiness and Hardship alternate steersmen—the Lyre and a light heart my fellow-passengers. Now, amid the giant waves of monopoly, the *solitary* loom is fast sinking. Thus must the Lyre, like a hencoop, be thrown on the wrecking waters, to float its owner ashore.

RHYMES.

THE BLIND BOY'S PRANKS.

["The following beautiful Stanzas are by a correspondent, who subscribes himself '*A Serf*,' and declares that he has to *weave fourteen hours out of the four-and-twenty*. We trust his *daily toil* will soon be abridged, that he may have more leisure to devote to an art in which he shows so much natural genius and cultivated taste."—*Aberdeen Herald*, Feb. 1841.]

> "I'll tell some ither time, quo' he,
> How we love an' laugh in the north countrie."
> Legend.

Men grew sae cauld, maids sae unkind,
   Love kentna whaur to stay.
Wi' fient an arrow, bow, or string,—
Wi' droopin' heart an' drizzled wing,
   He faught his lanely way.

Cauld, *cold*.   Ither, *other*.   Sae, *so*.
Faught, *battled*.   Kentna, *knew not*.   Whaur, *where*.
Fient, *deuce*.   Lanely, *lonely*.

"Is there nae mair, in Garioch fair,
    Ae spotless hame for me?
Hae politics, an' corn, an' kye,
Ilk bosom stappit? Fie, O fie!
    I'll swithe me o'er the sea."

He launched a leaf o' jessamine,
    On whilk he daured to swim,
An' pillowed his head on a wee rosebud,
Syne laithfu', lanely, Love 'gan scud
    Down Ury's* waefu' stream.

The birds sang bonnie as Love drew near,
    But dowie when he gaed by;
Till lull'd wi' the sough o' monie a sang,
He sleepit fu' soun' and sailed alang
    'Neath Heav'n's gowden sky!

'Twas just whaur creeping Ury greets
    Its mountain cousin Don,
There wandered forth a weelfaur'd deme,
    Wha listless gazed on the bonnie stream,
As it flirted an' played with a sunny beam
    That flickered its bosom upon.

Ae, *one.*	Kye, *cattle.*	Stappit, *crammed.*
Deme, *dame.*	Laithfu', *reluctant.*	Swithe, *hasten.*
Dowie, *sorrowfully.*	Mair, *more.*	Syne, *then.*
Fu' soun', *full sound.*	Monie, *many.*	Waefu', *woeful.*
Hae, *have.*	Nae, *no.*	Weelfaur'd, *well favoured*
Hame, *home.*	Sough, *sound.*	Whaur, *where.*

* The Ury, a small stream, at the junction of which with the Don stands Inver-Ury.

Love happit his head, I trow, that time,
 The jessamine bark drew nigh,
The lassie espied the wee rosebud,
An' aye her heart gae thud for thud,
 An' quiet it wadna lie.

"O gin I but had yon wearie wee flower
 That floats on the Ury sae fair!"
She lootit her hand for the silly rose-leaf,
But little wist she o' the pawkie thief,
 Was lurkin' an' laughin' there!

Love glower'd when he saw her bonnie dark e'e,
 An' swore by Heaven's grace
He ne'er had seen, nor thought to see,
Since e'er he left the Paphian lea,*
 Sae lovely a dwallin' place!

E'e, *eye.*	Happit, *covered.*	Wadna, *would not.*
Gae thud for thud, *gave beat for beat.*	Lootit, *put down.*	Wearie, *troublesome.*
	Pawkie, *sly.*	Wee, *little.*
Glower'd, *gazed wildly*		

---

* "Paphos, a very ancient city of Cyprus. It was celebrated for its beautiful temple of Venus, built on the spot where she landed when she rose from the sea. There were one hundred altars in her temple, which smoked daily, with a profusion of frankincense, and though exposed to the open air, they were never wetted by rain. Annual festivals were held here in honour of the goddess, and her oracle, which was connected with the temple, acquired for it considerable reputation."

Syne, first of a', in her blythesome breast,
   He built a bower, I ween;
An' what did the waefu' devilick neist?
But kindled a gleam like the rosy east,
   That sparkled frae baith her een.

An' then beneath ilk high e'e bree
   He placed a quiver there;
His bow? What but her shinin' brow?
An' O sic deadly strings he drew
   Frae out her silken hair.

Guid be our guard! sic deeds waur deen,
   Roun' a' our countrie then;
An' monie a hangin' lug was seen
'Mang farmers fat, an' lawyers lean,
   An' herds o' common men!

A', *all.*
Baith, *both.*
Bree, *brow.*
Deen, *done.*
Devilick, *imp.*

Een, *eyes.*
Frae, *from.*
Ilk, *each.*
Lug, *ear.*
Monie, *many.*

Neist, *next.*
Sic, *such.*
Syne, *then.*
Waefu', *teasing.*
Waur, *were.*

THE BLIND BOY'S PRANKS.

No. II.

Love roam'd awa frae Uryside,
    Wi' bow an' barbet keen,
Nor car'd a gowan whaur he gaed;
" Auld Scotland's mine, howe, heath, and glade,
    And I'll trock *that* wi' nane.

" Yon Ury damsel's diamond e'e,
    I've left it evermair;
She gied her heart unkent to me;
Now prees what wedded wichts maun pree,
    When I'm *un*priested there.

" That time by Ury's glowing stream,
    In sunny hour we met;
A lichter beild, a kinder hame
Than in the breast o' that fair dame,
    I'll never, never get.

Awa frae, *away from.*	Gied, *gave.*	Prees, *proves.*
Barbet, *arrow.*	Hame, *home.*	Trock, *barter.*
Beild, *shelter.*	Howe, *valley.*	Unkent, *unknown.*
Evermair, *evermore.*	Lichter, *lighter.*	Whaur, *whither.*
Gaed, *went.*	Maun, *must.*	Wichts, *worthies.*

"I kenn'd her meet wi' kindly say,
    A lov'd, a lowly name;
The heartless ruled poor Jean—an' they
Hae doom'd a loveless bride, for aye
    To busk a loveless hame.

"I'll seek bauld Benachie's proud pow,
    Grey king of common hills!
And try hoo bodies' hearts may lowe
Beneath thy shadeless, shaggy brow,
    Whaur dance a hundred rills."

Now trampin' bits, now fleein' miles,
    Frae aff the common road,
To keek at cadgers loupin' stiles,
Wha try the virtue an' the wiles
    Of maidens lichtly shod.

He passed Pittodrie's haunted wood,*
    Whaur devils dwalt langsyne;
He heard the Ury's timid flood,
An' Gadie's heigh an' hurrit scud,
    In playfu' sweetness twine.

Bauld, *bold.*	Hae, *have.*	Lichtly shod, *barefooted.*
Busk, *dress.*	Hoo, *how.*	
Cadgers, *country carriers.*	Keek, *look.*	Lowe, *blaze.*
	Kenn'd, *knew.*	Pow, *head.*
Heigh an' hurrit, *loud and rapid.*	Langsyne, *long ago.*	Say, *words.*
	Loupin', *leaping.*	Whaur, *where.*

---

* Among the many pretty legends and stories that affix to almost every hill and water, wood and howe of the Garioch, the following is often heard:—Upon a time far, far gone by, a Caledonian

An' there he saw (for Love has een,
  Tho' whiles nae gleg at seein')
He saw an' kenn'd a kind auld frien',
Wha wander'd ghaistlike an' alane,
  Forsaken, shunn'd, an' deein'.

Auld, *old.* Ghaistlike, *ghostlike.* Nae gleg at seein', *not*
Deein', *dying.* Kenn'd, *knew.*   *quicksighted.*

---

demon took a fancy, to amuse himself awhile in the neighbourhood of Benachie—a portion of our world he had scarcely looked upon since the bloody game of Harlaw. To put matters astirring again in his own way, he took a stroll into the woods of Pittodrie. There let him walk, while we take a hasty look at those upon whom he is said to have recommenced his dark doings.

The boasted beauty of five parishes was the "Maiden of Drumdurno." A farmer's only daughter she—a cantie, clever, hame-bred Scotch lassie. Three notions, in particular, appear to have held uppermost keeping in her bonnie brow—to-wit, that her father had the sharpest outlook, Benachie the highest *tap,* and her ain Jamie, the kindest heart in the whole world.

Aware (and why not?) of her own personal loveliness, she wisely made all within as fair and fitting. She lived a creature full of soul —her breast the tenement of love and happiness—gaiety and tenderness hovered in her eye, like watchful spirits, ready to minister— waiting, as it were, just to see what was wanted—a laugh or a tear. Many, many had wooed—one, at last, had won her. The unsuccessful went, each according to his way, in these cases—some sighing, some drawing comfort from a new purpose, some from an old pipe— all, however, wishing happy days to the betrothed "Maiden of Drumdurno." One alone—one fed the hope of vengeance—one grim, horse-shoe-hearted rascal of a smith. Parish smith and precentor, too, he was. This rejected ruffian watched that night in Pittodrie woods, in thought that "Jamie" would, as usual, in leaving Drumdurno, pass that way. "Oh, that my eternal destruction could plague their earthly peace," cried he, "how soon and sure the bargain would be mine!" "Capital wish!" cried the seducer of Eve, "I'll do the thing for you on your own conditions." Perpetual vassalage on the part of the "red wud" smith—written desolation to the

Her look ance gay as gleams o' gowd
  Upon a silvery sea;
Now dark an' dowie as the cloud
That creeps athwart yon leafless wood,
  In cauld December's e'e.

Dowie, *cheerless.*   Nae, *no.*

---

luckless lovers of Drumdurno, was compact and settlement that night, in the black woods of Pittodrie. * * * The bonniest and the blythest lass within sight of Benachie was drifting up the bridal baking—and the bridal and the bannocks "baith her ain." "It sets ye weel to work, lass, gin ye had onie mair speed at it." This compound of taunt and compliment was uttered by a stranger, who had been hanging on about the kitchen, the last hour or so—a queer, rollicking, funny, lump of a "roader," and, by his own story, in search of work. "I kenna whether it sets me or no," quoth the maiden, "but I think nane could grudge wi' my speed." It is clear by this, that the complimentary portion of the stranger's remark had found its way. Alas! the pitiable truth! Alas! for humanity! When it *would* be flattered, the poison is more surely imparted beneath the roughest coverture. In faulting that which is blameless, the flatterer assumes the hue and weight of honesty, and works securely there.

The jest and banter was exchanged, with mingled glee and earnestness, till at length the lass, all thoughtlessly, was inveigled into the fatal wager. The terms of that fearful agreement are stated at varied points of the horrible. The most temperate reciters insist that HE undertook to "lay" a road from bottom to top of Benachie ere she baked up her firlot of meal. The forfeiture hazarded on his part is not on record. Most likely the light-hearted, happy bride regarded the whole as one of the merry jokes that rang from that merry old man, and heeded not exacting conditions in a matter she conceived to be impossible. Her part of the pledge, however, was, " that she became his *own* if the road is laid ere the meal be baken." * * * Now, now, the last bannock is on the girdle, but for the past hour her mind was filling, in the gush of that tearful sweetness that pours o'er the heart of a willing bride, so the hill, the road, the wager, old man and all—all were forgotten—all overshaded that

Hear ye the heartsick soun's that fa'
  Frae lips that bless nae mair?
Like beildless birdies when they ca'
Frae wet, wee wing the batted snaw,
  Her sang soughs o' despair.

Song of the Forsaken.

My cheek is faded sair, love,
    An' lichtless fa's my e'e;
My breast a' lane and bare, love,
    Has aye a beild for thee.

An' lichtless fa's my e'e, *my look is disregarded.*
Batted, *hardened.*
Beild, *shelter.*
Beildless, unsheltered.
Ca', *shake off.*
Fa', *fall.*
Frae, *from.*
Lane, *lone.*
Mair, *more.*
Soughs, *sounds.*
Soun's, *sounds.*

---

shared of earth—but *one*—one only, one darling thought. The hour of tryst was near. The lowering, gloomy-like fall of the night dismayed her, and she looked wistfully at the cloud settling on the hill. "Its nae *that*, nor mony siclike 'll gar him bide frae me; but I'm wae to see him weet. God of my heart," she cried, "what's yon I see!" * * * The road is to be seen to this day. She fled towards the woods of Pittodrie, pursued. The prayer she could not utter was answered. With the last bound the demon grasped a stone. Such the transformed bride. So she stands there even now.

And quick the pace, and quick the pulse,
    Wha wanders there alane,
Atween Pittodrie's drearie wood
    An' the dowie "maiden's stane."

My breast, though lane and bare,
The hame o' cauld despair,
Yet ye 've a dwallin' there,
    A' darksome though it be.

Yon guarded roses glowin',
    Its wha daur min't to pu'?
But aye the wee bit gowan
    Ilk reckless hand may strew.
An' aye the wee, wee gowan,
Unsheltered, lanely growin',
Unkent, uncared its ruin,
    Sae marklessly it grew.

An' am I left to rue, then,
    Wha ne'er kent Love but thee;
An' gae a love as true, then,
    As woman's heart can gie?
But can ye cauldly view,
A bosom burstin' fu'?
An' hae ye broken noo,
    The heart ye *sought* frae me?

Cauldly, *coldly*.	Ilk, *each*.	Sae, *so*.
Daur, *dare*.	Kent, *knew*.	Unkent, *unknown*.
Dwallin', *house*.	Lanely, *lonely*.	We bit gowan, *little field daisy*.
Gae, *gave*.	Min't, *venture*.	
Gie, *give*.	Pu', *pluck*.	Wha, *who*.

THE BLIND BOY'S PRANKS.

No. III.

By the lowe o' a lawyer's ingle bricht,
  Wi' gruesome looks an' dark,
The Deil sat pickin' his thum's ae nicht
  Frae evendoun want o' wark.
At length in the learn'd lug to hark
  He cannilie screw'd him roun',
Syne claw'd his elbow an' leuch to mark
  The lang-leaft buik brocht doun.

Wi' outshot een, o'er leaf an' line,
  Sae keenly did they leuk,
An' oh! there was ae waefu' sign
  Within that wearie buik,

Ae, *one*.
Bricht, *bright*.
Buik, *book*.
Cannilie, *slily*.
Chiel, *fellow*.
Evendoun, *downright*.
Frae, *from*.
Gruesome, *loathsome*.
Hark, *whisper*.
Ingle, *chimney corner*.
Lang-leaft buik brocht doun, *ledger brought down*.
Leuk, *look*.
Leuch, *laughed*.
Lowe, *blaze*.
Lug, *ear*.
Nicht, *night*.
Sae, *so*.
Syne, *then*.
Waeful, *woeful*.
Wearie, *troublesome*.
Wark, *work*.

Whan Hornie gae his mou a cruik
　　An' whisper'd, " Look ye, here's
A crafter* carl upon our hook
　　Ahint these twa 'ha'f years.'

" Gae harry him, man, an' gar him dee
　　The lave is your's an' mine;
His daisy dochter's scornfu' e'e
　　Will blink less saucy syne.
In beinless wa's just lat her pine,
　　Sic lanesome hardships pree;
An' here's my loof the haughty quean
　　Will fa' afore she flee."

Love heard, an' skonnart wi' the plot
　　Swore grey the very moon,
That he would hae the lawyer shot,
　　An' gar the ither droun.
He flaft his wing o'er brae, an' boun'
　　O'er field and forest wide;
In lowly biggin lichted doun
　　An' knelt by Annie's side.

Ahint these twa 'ha'f years, *behind in his rent two terms.*	Cruik, *twist.*	In, *within.*
	Daisy, *darling.*	Lanesome, *lonely.*
	Dochter, *daughter.*	Lave, *rest.*
Beinless wa's, *comfortless walls.*	Droun, *drown.*	Loof, *hand.*
	Flaft, *flapp'd.*	Mou, *mouth.*
Biggin, *building.*	Gae harry, *go ruin.*	Pree, *prove.*
Blink, *look.*	Gar him dee, *make him die.*	Sic, *such.*
Boun', *bounded.*		Skonnart, *disgusted.*
Crafter carl, *crofter man.*	Gar, *make.*	Syne, *then.*
	Hae, *have.*	

---

* A crofter is one who holds a four or five acre piece of land, and house.

THE BLIND BOY'S PRANKS.

O, whaur is love maist lovely seen?
   In timorous glances stealing—
Half-hid, half-own'd, in diamond e'en
   The soul-fraught look revealing?
No; see it there—a daughter kneeling
   A father's sickbed near,
With uprais'd heart to heaven appealing,
   That—*that's* the look for angel's wear!

Annie, sic look was thine that nicht,
   Yon waesome watchfu' hour;
The man o' buiks thow'd at the sicht—
   He tint a' pith an' pow'r.
Auld Hornie then forthwith 'gan scour
   By heicht an' howe—an' then
At Cardin's brig* he tumbl't o'er
   An' never raise again.

The lanefu' lawyer held his breath,
   An' word micht utter nane;
But lookit aye—grew aye mair laith
   To blaud her bonnie een.

Blaud, *blear.*
Buiks, *books.*
Heicht an' howe, *hill and dale.*
Lanefu', *forlorn.*
Mair laith, *more loath.*
Micht, *might.*
Nicht, *night.*
Pith, *strength.*
Raise, *rose.*
Sic, *such.*
Sicht, *sight.*
Thow'd, *melted.*
Tint a', *lost all.*
Waesome, *dreary.*

---

* Cardin's brig over the Gadie, to the west of Logie, Elphinstone.

Love threw a shaft, sae sure an' keen,
   It trembled in his heart;
An' micht I deem, altho' a stane
   Had dwallin' in the part.

Syne, slow an' dowie, wending hame,
   Wi' cares unkent afore,
His heart a' sinkin' doun wi' shame—
   Wi' new love gushin' o'er.
By buik or bond he held nae store,
   For bound eneuch was he;
Nor could he read aucht ither lore
   Than beam'd in yon bricht e'e.

A saftness hangs on ilka word;
   A wish on ilka hour;
A sang is soucht fra' every bird,
   A sich frae every flower.
Now briefs forsaken, rot an' sour—
   A sonnet rules a summons;
E'en Blackstone's weighty wit maun cour
   To far mair weighty woman's.

Aucht ither, *ought other*.
Bricht e'e, *bright eye*.
Ilka, *every*.
Mair, *more*.
Maun cour, *must yield*.
Sich, *sigh*.
Syne, *then*.
Unkent afore, *unknown before*.
Wending hame, *wandering home*.

LINES

OCCASIONED BY THE SUDDEN DEATH OF COUNT JOHN LESLIE OF BALQUHAIN AND FETTERNEIR.

August, 1844.

Beloved by all—cut off in the dawn of manhood—he was borne to the grave by a weeping tenantry.

Oh, why? but God alone knows why—
Do churls cling aye to earth;
While the brave and the just, and the generous die,
The hour that owns their worth?
    Alas! and woe!—so sad—so true,
    The blink that's brightest—briefest too.

'T was a dolfu' dawn yon morning saw
On the turrets of brown Balquhain;

Blink, *beam.*

When the Leslie lay on red Harlaw
" Wi' his six good sons a' slain."*
    But nane less leal the sigh and the tear,
    And the waesome hearts 'round Fetterneir.

Waesome, sorrowful.

---

* In 1411, Donald of the Isles marched towards Aberdeen, the inhabitants of which were in dreadful alarm at the near approach of this marauder and his fierce hordes; but their fears were allayed by the speedy appearance of a well-equipped army, commanded by the Earl of Mar, who bore a high military character, assisted by many brave knights and gentlemen in Angus and the Mearns. Advancing from Aberdeen, Mar marched by Inverury, and descried the Highlanders stationed at the village of Harlaw, on the water of Ury near its junction with the Don. Mar soon saw that he had to contend with tremendous odds, but although his forces were, it is said, as one to ten to that opposed to him, he resolved, from the confidence he had in his steel-clad knights, to risk a battle. Having placed a small but select body of knights and men-at-arms in front, under the command of the constable of Dundee and the sheriff of Angus, the Earl drew up the main strength of his army in the rear, including the Murrays, the Straitons, the Maules, the Irvings, the Lesleys, the Lovels, the Stirlings, headed by their respective chiefs. The Earl then placed himself at the head of this body. At the head of the Islesmen and Highlanders was the Lord of the Isles, subordinate to whom were Mackintosh and Maclean and other Highland chiefs, all bearing the most deadly hatred to their Saxon foes. On a signal being given, the Highlanders and Islesmen, setting up those terrific shouts and yells which they were accustomed to raise on entering into battle, rushed forward upon their opponents; but they were received with great firmness and bravery by the knights, who, with their spears levelled, and battle-axes raised, cut down many of their impetuous but badly armed adversaries. After the Lowlanders had recovered themselves from the shock which the furious onset of the Highlanders had produced, Sir James Scrymgeour, at the head of the knights and bannerets who fought under him, cut his way through the thick columns of the Islesmen, carrying death every where around him; but the slaughter of hundreds by this brave party did not intimidate the Highlanders, who kept pouring in by thousands to supply the place of those who had fallen. Surrounded on all sides, no alternative remained for Sir James and his valorous companions but victory or death, and the latter was their lot. The

Don's waters deftly wandered on,
Sae wantonly and sae clear;
And dazzling danced beneath the sun
That gleam'd o'er Fetterneir.
 While the lov'd of the land is bounding away,
 Like his own bold stream—to the risen day.

---

constable of Dundee was amongst the first who suffered, and his fall so encouraged the Highlanders, that seizing and stabbing the horses, they thus unhorsed their riders, whom they despatched with their daggers. In the mean time the Earl of Mar, who had penetrated with his main army into the very heart of the enemy, kept up the unequal contest with great bravery, and, although he lost during the action almost the whole of his army, he continued the fatal struggle with a handful of men till nightfall. The disastrous result of this battle was one of the greatest misfortunes which had ever happened to the numerous respectable families in Angus and the Mearns. Many of these families lost not only their head, but every male in the house. Andrew Lesley, third Laird of Balquhain, is said to have fallen, with six of his sons (the *Laurus Lesleana* says eleven, and that he himself fell some years after in a battle at Brakoe, killed by the sheriff of Angus, 1420.) Isabel Mortimer, his wife, founded a chaplainry in the Chapel of Garioch, and built a cross called Leslie's Cross, to their memory. Besides Sir James Scrymgeour, Sir Alexander Ogilvy, the sheriff of Angus, with his eldest son George Ogilvy, Sir Thomas Murray, Sir Robert Maule of Panmure, Sir Alexander Irving of Drum, Sir William Abernethy of Salton, Sir Alexander Straiton of Lauriston, James Lovel, and Alexander Stirling, and Sir Robert Davidson, provost of Aberdeen, with five hundred men-at-arms, including the principal gentry of Buchan, and the greater part of the burgesses of Aberdeen who followed their provost, were among the slain. The Highlanders left nine hundred men dead on the field of battle, including the chiefs, Maclean and Mackintosh. This memorable battle was fought on the eve of the feast of St. James the Apostle, the 24th day of July, in the year 1411, " and from the ferocity with which it was contested, and the dismal spectacle of civil war and bloodshed exhibited to the country, it appears to have made a deep impression on the national mind. It fixed itself in the music and the poetry of Scotland; a march, called ' the Battle of Harlaw,' continued to be a popular air down to the time of Drum-

O bid him bide—ye birdies that sing!—
Or bid him nae fend sae fast—
Haud back your tears ye witchfu' spring
Wha's waters weird his last.*

     Fay, *foredoomed*.

---

mond of Hawthornden, and a spirited ballad, on the same event, is still repeated in our age, describing the meeting of the armies, and the deaths of the chiefs, in no ignoble strain." Mar and the few brave companions in arms who survived the battle, were so exhausted with fatigue and the wounds they received, that they were obliged to pass the night on the field of battle, where they expected a renewal of the attack next morning; but when morning dawned, they found that the Lord of the Isles had retreated, during the night, by Inverury and the hill of Benachie. To pursue him was impossible, and he was therefore allowed to retire, without molestation, and to recruit his exhausted strength. The site of the battle is thus described in the manuscript Geographical Description of Scotland collected by Macfarlane, and preserved in the Advocates' Library [Vol. i. p. 7.]: "Through this parish (the Chapel of Garioch, formerly called Capella Beatæ Mariæ Virginis de Garryoch) runs the king's highway from Aberdeen to Inverness, and from Aberdeen to the high country. A large mile to the east of the church lies the field of an ancient battle called the battle of Harlaw, from a country town of that name hard by. This town, and the field of battle, which lies along the king's highway upon a moor, extending a short mile from south-east to north-west, stands on the north-east side of the water of Urie, and a small distance therefrom. To the west of the field of battle, about half a mile, is a farmer's house called Legget's Den, hard by, in which is a tomb, built in the form of a malt-steep, of four large stones, covered with a broad stone above, where, as the country people generally report, Donald of the Isles lies buried, being slain in the battle, and therefore they call it commonly Donald's Tomb." This is an evident mistake, as it is well known that Donald was not slain. Mr. Tytler conjectures with much probability that the tomb alluded to may be that of the chief of Maclean or Mackintosh, and he refers, in support of this opinion, to Macfarlane's Genealogical Collections, in which an account is given of the family of Maclean, and from which it appears

---

* The Count's death was occasioned by his incautiously drinking cold spring water, he being then over-heated, whilst shooting on the hills.

> But away and away—he bodes a bier,
> For the woods look fay 'round Fetterneir. *
>
> We lend no lay to living man—
> Nor sing for fee or fear;
> Our cheek tho' pale, yet never faun'
> The stain of a mimic tear.
>> In *truth* we mourn the bud that sprung,
>> Unblossom'd—blighted—fair and young.

---

that Lauchlan Lubanich had, by Macdonald's daughter, a son, called Eachin Rusidh ni Cath, or Hector Rufus Bellicosus, who commanded as lieutenant-general under the Earl of Ross at the battle of Harlaw, when he and Irving of Drum, seeking out one another by their armorial bearings on their shields, met and killed each other. This Hector was married to a daughter of the Earl of Douglas.

* Fetterneir, once a summer seat of the bishops of Aberdeen. Wallace is said to have slept there one night; hence part of it is called Wallace's Tower. At the Reformation this manor was given to the Lesleys of Balquhain (pronounced Balwine), for their assistance to the Earl of Huntly in protecting the Cathedral of Aberdeen from the fury of the Reformers. It is the burial-place of the Lesleys.

The family of the Lesleys is five hundred and eighty years' standing; Sir George, the founder, having got the lands of Balquhain from King David the Second in 1340. There had been four counts of this family, the last now living (1650) at the Emperor's court. The first of these counts was Walter, youngest son to John, tenth laird of Balquhain, by his third wife, who having, in A.D. 1634, killed Count Wallenstein, the Emperor's general, was made a colonel of the Guards, created Count Lesley, Field Marshal, Privy Councillor, Governor of Sclavonia, and by Leopold the First sent ambassador to Constantinople, having just before been made Knight of the Golden Fleece. He died in 1667, at Vienna.

About half a mile to the south-east of the church is to be seen the old ruinous Castle of Balquhain. In it Queen Mary spent a day on her journey to the north, which terminated in the battle of Corrichie. The only remains of the building are a few shattered fragments of the court or quadrangle of which it at one time consisted, and the noble square tower or keep, which was erected about the year 1530 to replace the more ancient castle, which had been burned down in a memorable feud with the Forbeses in the year 1526.

WHISPERINGS FOR THE UNWASHED.

"Tyrants make not slaves—slaves make tyrants."

SCENE—A Town in the North.   TIME—Six o'clock morning.
Enter TOWN DRUMMER.*

RUBADUB, rubadub, row-dow-dow!
The sun is glinting on hill and knowe,
An' saft the pillow to the fat man's pow—
Sae fleecy an' warm the guid "*hame-made*,"
An' cozie the happin o' the farmer's bed.
The feast o' yestreen how it oozes through,
In bell an' blab on his burly brow.
Nought recks he o' drum an' bell,
The girnal's fou an' sure the "sale;"

Bell an' blab, *sweat drop*.
Fou, *full*.
Girnal, *meal bin*.
Glinting, *beaming*.
Hame-made, *blanket*
Happin, *covering*.
Knowe, *knoll*.
Laird, *landlord*.
Pow, *head*.
Yestreen, *last night*.

---

* In most of the small boroughs of the north of Scotland there is a town drummer, who parades at five in the summer and six o'clock in the winter. In Nairn a man blows a cow-horn.

The laird an' he can crap an keep*—
Weel, weel may he laugh in his gowden sleep.
His dream abounds in stots, or full
Of cow an' corn, calf an' bull;
Of cattle shows, of dinner speaks—
Toom, torn, and patch'd like weavers' breeks;
An' sic like meaning hae, I trow,
As rubadub, rubadub, row-dow-dow.

Rubadub, rubadub, row-dow-dow!
Hark, how he waukens the Weavers now!
Wha lie belair'd in a dreamy steep—
A mental swither 'tween death an' sleep—
Wi' hungry wame and hopeless breast,
Their food no feeding, their sleep no rest.
Arouse ye, ye sunken, unravel your rags,
No coin in your coffers, no meal in your bags;
Yet cart, barge, and waggon, with load after load,
Creak mockfully, passing your breadless abode.
The stately stalk of Ceres bears,
But not for you, the bursting ears;
In vain to you the lark's lov'd note,
For you no summer breezes float,
Grim winter through your hovel pours—
Dull, din, and healthless vapour yours.

Crap, *crop*.	Hae, *have*.	Toom, *shallow*.
Belair'd, *stuck*.	Stots, *young cattle*.	Wame, *belly*.
Din, *noise*.	Swither, *hesitation*.	

* Had Heaven intended corn to be the property of *one* class only, corn would grow in *one land* only, and only on one stem. But corn is the child of every soil; its grains and its stems are numberless as the tears of the hungry. The wide spread bounty of God was never willed to be a wide spread sorrow to man.

The nobler Spider* weaves alone,
And feels the little web his *own*,
His hame, his fortress, foul or fair,
Nor factory whipper swaggers there.
Should ruffian wasp, or flaunting fly
Touch his lov'd lair, 'T IS TOUCH AND DIE!
Supreme in rags, ye weave, in tears,
The shining robe your murderer wears;
Till worn, at last, to very "*waste*,"
A hole to die in, at the best;
And, dead, the session saints begrudge ye
The twa-three deals in death to lodge ye;
They grudge the grave wherein to drap ye,
An' grudge the very *muck* to hap ye.

* * * * * * *

Deals, *boards for a coffin.* Muck, *dirt.* Waste, *in weavers' language broken threads.*
Hap, *cover.* Session saints, *elders.*

---

* It was at Inverury, after losing seven battles against the English, that Robert Bruce, lying ill in his bed, marked a spider, which was endeavouring to mount to the ceiling, fall down seven times, but on the eighth attempt succeed. The Scotch and English army were just preparing for battle, when Bruce, inspired by this omen, rose, and heading his dispirited troops, after a desperate struggle succeeded in routing the enemy, and laid the foundation of a series of successes against the usurping invader, which secured the glory and independence of the kingdom of Scotland. The welcome he received at Inverury, in his dark hour of distress, induced him to bestow on it the privileges of a royal burgh.

Nor is this the only time that the spider has influenced the destiny of kingdoms. In our own times the careful investigation of their habits in different weather, by a prisoner in his dungeon, afforded the indices upon which Dumourier invaded and overrun Holland in 1797.

Rubadub, rubadub, row-dow-dow!
The drunkard clasps his aching brow;
And there be they, in their squalor laid,
The supperless brood on loathsome bed;
Where the pallid mother croons to rest,
The withering babe at her milkless breast.
She, wakeful, views the risen day
Break gladless o'er her home's decay,
And God's blest light a ghastly glare
Of grey and deathy dimness there.
In all things near, or sight or sounds,
Sepulchral rottenness abounds;
Yet he, the sovereign filth, will prate,
In stilted terms, of Church and State,
As things that *he* would mould anew—
Could all but his brute self subdue.
Ye vilest of the crawling things,
Lo! how well the fetter clings
To recreant collar! Oh, may all
The self-twined lash unbroken fall,
Nor hold until our land is free'd
Of craven, crouching slugs, that breed
In fetid holes, and, day by day,
Yawn their unliving life away!
But die they will not, cannot—why?
They live not—therefore, cannot die.
In soul's dark deadness dead are they,
Entomb'd in thick corkswollen clay.

Brood, *family.*   **Croons,** *groans.*   **Sovereign filth,** *drunkard.*
Corkswollen, *beery.*

What tho' they yield their fulsome breath,
The change but mocks the name of death!
Existence, skulking from the sun,
In misery many, in meanness one.
When brave hearts would the fight renew,
Hope, weeping, withering points to you!

    Arouse ye, but neither with bludgeon nor blow,
Let *mind* be your armour, *darkness* your foe;
'T is not in the ramping of demagogue rage,
Nor yet in the mountebank patriot's page,
In sounding palaver, nor pageant, I ween,
In blasting of trumpet, nor vile tambourine;
For these are but mockful and treacherous things—
The thorns that "crackle" to sharpen their stings.
When fair Science gleams over city and plain,
When Truth walks abroad all unfetter'd again,
When the breast glows to Love and the brow beams in Light—
Oh! hasten it Heaven! MAN LONGS FOR HIS RIGHT.

THE MANIAC MOTHER'S DREAM.

When sunlight leaves the lea,
    And songless birds would rest,
When sleeping dews there be
    Upon the gowan's breast,—
Who, like the dark'ning west,
    That lone one? Who is she?
'T is sorrow's fated guest,
    And *this* her revelry :—

Through crumbling tombs, o'er boneless graves,
The wrathful wind in that hour that raves,
Shall mingling, mingling, moan and sigh,
To the maniac mother's lullaby;
While cow'ring 'neath the ruined wall
Of Elgin's dark Cathedral.*

---

* This venerable and magnificent relic of cathedral grandeur is situated in Elgin, Morayshire, on the banks of the river Lossie. It was built early in the thirteenth century. About a hundred and fifty years after the foundation, it was entirely burned down by the ruffian son of a Scottish king. The creature—a common destroyer—lives yet in hateful record, as "The Wolf of Badenoch."

"The cathedral is surrounded by a burying-ground, one of the largest churchyards, perhaps, in Great Britain. In it are interred

As o'er her burning brow
　She laves yon holy spring,
And down her cheek of snow
　The big tear mingling—
Would some mild spirit bring
　The heart-wrung living gem,
And place it sparkling
　In sorrow's diadem!

---

the remains of many distinguished persons, including several of the kings of Scotland. The churchyard is enclosed by a stone wall. What with the number of graves, the beauty and variety of the sculptured memorials of departed worth and greatness, and the grandeur of the dilapidated cathedral,—a building which is, indeed, pre-eminently magnificent, even in ruins,—the scene is calculated to make a strong impression on the spectator."

It is not all of its early grandeur, nor of its latter desolation, its splendour nor its ruin—not all the historian has told or antiquarian minuted—will impart an interest to the spot, like what it derives now from a maniac—an outcast mother and her orphan boy. It fell out thus:—In 1745, Marjory Gillan, a young woman, resided in Elgin—she was well connected and goodlooking—was privately married to a young man who had enlisted in a regiment then quartered in the town—she went abroad with her husband, followed by the bitter reproach of her relatives and friends, who considered the step she had taken a discredit and an affront to all connected. In the same spirit of unrelenting harshness was she received on her return, which occurred about two years from the time she left. It was rumoured that her husband had used her ill, had left her behind, and was killed in battle. The forlorn one now sought her homeless native place, unsettled in mind, and carrying a baby in her arms. "The reception she met with, and the wild fancies of a wandering mind, induced her to take a strange step. Amidst the crumbling ruins of the cathedral, there is one chamber still entire; a small, cellar-like room, about five feet square, with scarcely any light, and which is said, in ancient times, to have been the sacristy, or place for keeping the vessels used in the offices of religion. Here the poor outcast took up her abode, rendered insensible, by her obscured reason, to the nocturnal horrors of a place which, in a better state of

Well might the sallow goddess wear
In her cold coronal that tear!
The tear of tears is hers, all shed
On sireless son's unsheltered head.

---

mind, she would have dreaded to approach after dusk. There was in this room an ancient sculptured font, which she used as a bed to her infant; other furniture she had none. When it was known that she had gone to reside in this dismal place, the people felt as if it were an imputation against their Christian feelings. She and her babe were repeatedly carried, by some one or other of them, to their houses, but she always made her way back to the sacristy. At length, finding her determined to live there, they contented themselves with giving her food and alms, and for several years she wandered about with her boy, under the appellation of '*Daft May Gilzean*'*—a harmless creature, that wept and sang by turns. Her lover or husband was no more heard of in the country, although he had several relations living in the neighbourhood, with whom he might have been expected to correspond, if he had remained in life. Andrew Anderson, the son of May Gilzean, grew up in all the raggedness and misery which might be expected under such circumstances to fall to his lot. It is questionable if he ever knew the comforts of a bed, or of a cooked meal of any kind, till his boyhood was far advanced. The one solacement of his forlorn existence was the affection which his mother always continued to feel for him."† Daft May dies—Andrew Anderson, her ragged and bewildered boy, is forced, by ungracious treatment from an uncle with whom he dwelt, to cast himself upon the world. Fortunately he had obtained some education gratuitously in his native place. With this, his only wealth, "he made his way to Leith, and thence to London, where he was taken into the workshop of a tailor, who, finding that he wrote neatly and had a knowledge of accounts, began, after some time, to employ him as a clerk. He was one day commissioned to take home a suit of clothes to a military gentleman, and to grant a discharge for the account. This gentleman was himself a Scotsman, and bore a commission in a regiment about to proceed to the East Indies. He was, like all Scotsmen *at a distance from home*, interested

---

* The *z* in this name is not pronounced.
† Chambers' Edinburgh Journal, No. 385.

When misery's guideless gush is o'er,
And drowning reason speaks no more;
When broken, withered, one by one,
All, all earth-bounded wish is gone;
When *woe* is wearied, nor can tell
On the scaithed breast another knell;
Oh! mother's heart, up-welling there
Affection wrestles with despair,
And measureless that burning flow,
A mother's heart alone may know.

* * * *

" Bairnie, mine, be hush'd to me,
An' I'll tell you a dream that I dreamt o' thee,

---

in hearing his native tongue spoken, by however humble a person. When, in addition to this, he observed the pleasing countenance and manners of the youth, and found that the discharge appended by him to the account was in a good regular hand, he entered into conversation, asked whence he came, what were his prospects, and other such questions, and finally inquired if he would like to go abroad as a soldier and officer's servant. Anderson required little persuasion to induce him to enter into the stranger's views. He enlisted as a private, and immediately after set sail with the regiment, in the capacity of drummer, acting at the same time, according to previous agreement, as the valet or servant of his patron." A singularly marked Providence guided the footsteps of " Daft May's loonie," and, after an absence of sixty years, he returned to the place of his nativity the renowned and wealthy Lieutenant-General Anderson of the East India Company's Service. He " founded and endowed, within the burgh of Elgin, an hospital for the maintenance of indigent men and women not under fifty years of age; also a school of industry for the maintenance and education of male and female children of the labouring classes, whose parents are unable to maintain and educate them, and for putting out the said children, when fit to be so, as apprentices to some trade or occupation, or employing them in such a manner as may enable them to earn a livelihood by their lawful industry, and make them useful members of society."

THE MANIAC MOTHER'S DREAM.

As we lay in the lythe o' yon bare graif-stane—
Oh, me! 'twas an unco dream yestreen;
Yon gruesome spirit that haunts our hame,
Wi' ither eldrich goblins came;
They pu'd my heart, and they dimm'd my e'e,
Till my baby bairn I cou'dna see:
But aye I heard your waesome cry,
As they bore me o'er yon dreamy sky;
And weel, frae the height o' my heavenly ha',
On sorrowin' earth my bairn I saw;
I saw you conjured—kent your greet,
As you crouch'd and cower'd at the carlin's feet;
Ilk tear that sped frae your sleepless e'e
Were draps like the livin' bleed frae me,
Till toil'd, and torn, and wan, and wae,
Ye wandered far frae your heather brae;
The shrifted souls that dwelt wi' me,
Looked wistfu' o'er your destiny;
And oh! to me their holy sang
In changefu' sweetness swelled alang;
And aye their godward melody
Breathed watchfu' benisons on thee.
I saw the warl' gang rowin' by,
And *you* beneath its kindest sky;
I marked the hue o' crimson weir,
Bedeck the breast o' my bairnie dear;

Benisons, *blessings.*   Greet, *to weep, cry.*   Rowin', *rolling.*
Bleed, *blood.*   Gruesome, *loathsome.*   Wae, *sad.*
Carlin, *old woman.*   Ilk, *each.*   Warl', *world.*
Eldrich, *hideous.*   Ither, *other.*   Weir, *war.*
Frae, *from.*   Kent, *knew.*   Wistfu', *anxious.*
Gang, *go.*

Till the highest head in yon jewelled land,
Bent to the beck o' my Andrew's hand.
Ae time the warld came rowin' by,
We missed ye in yon lo'esome sky,
But tracked your keel across the main,
To your hameless Highland braes again,
And bonnie was the bough and fair
Your brave hand brought and planted there!
Braid, braid its branch o' fadeless green,
Wi' streaks o' sunny light between,
As, laughing frae their yellow sky,
They kissed the leaves that loot them by.
There smiling Plenty safely laid
In Mercy's lap her gowden head;
The fiercest winter winds that rair,
Could never fauld a sna'-wreath there;
E'en misery's cauld and witherin' e'e
Fell feckless o'er your stately tree.
The stricken deer weel there might rest,
And lap the bleed frae its dapple breast;
The wingless doo would leap and splash
A' drippin' frae the hunter's flash,
Safe shelter'd in yon shady fa',
To croon its little heart awa';
And wee, wee birdies, nane could name,
Came flutterin' there, and found a hame;

Ae, *one*.
Bleed, *blood*.
Braid, *broad*.
Cauld, *cold*.
Croon, *moan*.
Doo, *dove*.

Fauld, *fold*.
Feckless, *feebly*.
Frae, *from*.
Loot, *let*.
Rair, *to roar*.

Rowin', *rolling*.
Sna'-wreath, *snow-wreath*.
Wee, *small, little*.
Weel, *well*.

E'en rooks and ravens, tired o' bleed,
Sought shelter there in time o' need.
But, oh! that wind, its harrying scream
Reive through the rest o' my bonnie dream."

Harrying, *ruinous.* **Reive,** *tore.*

OLD FATHER FROST AND HIS FAMILY.

GRIM father Frost, he hath children twain,
The cloud-born daughters of Lady Rain;
The elder, a coquettish pattering thing,
Would woo you in winter, and pelt you in spring;
At times you might scarce feel her feathery fall,
Anon she will beard you with icicle ball;
When the warrings of heaven roll higher and higher,
She, coward-like, flees from the conflict of fire—

---

* Ere yet the schoolmaster was so much abroad, the schoolmistress was very much at home. In Aberdeen, about thirty years ago, at any of fifty lowly firesides, could be found one of those simple academies yclept a "Wifie's Squeel." In one of these was imparted to me all the tuition I ever received in the way of letters—gatherings in after-life being only "crumbs from the rich man's table." *Our* Wifie had always twenty scholars, one cat, one *taurds*, and one opinion. The scholars exercised her patience, the cat her affections, and the opinion, simply that the *taurds* (a cordovan improvement on the feebler birch) was, as an exercise, the best panacea on earth for rheumatism in the right shoulder. When Elspet Gillespie wanted a bit of exercise in this way, there was no long waiting for a defaulter to give a duty-like interest to her emotions. The evolutions of the *taurds* then awakened some excitement throughout the establishment, accompanied by strong marks of disapproval in the party honoured by her immediate regard, and stirred curious sympathies even in those who sat by in safety—

Taurds, *a leather strap.*

Yet heightens the havoc, for her feeble power,
Tho' scaithless the oak, how it fells the frail flower!
And the bud of the berry, the bloom of the bean,
Are founder'd to earth by the merciless quean;

Quean, *wench, jade.*

---

if, indeed, safety could be coupled with such an hour. When the pangs of rheumatism were lulled by a sense of weariness about the shoulder blade, Elspet resumed her proud elevation above the trembling assembly, who felt there was one great woman in the world, and there sat she. Boys five years old and upwards brought the fee of three "bawbees" and a peat weekly. Our junior class was composed of little ones, who were too young to talk, but who, of course, made most noise. These were charged sixpence. I cannot say what portion of that sum was entered to "din." She had, indeed, much trouble with these, and longer time of it, having to tend them during the whole day, until their poor mothers returned from the spinning-mill or the field. The outfit for grown-up *students* was a Bible, a Westminster Catechism, and a stool, all of which were removed on Saturday, and fetched again on Monday. Oh, that I could tell, and tell it rightly, the "skailing of the squeel!" or paint yon joyous little mob, gushing forth from the *laigh* door of Elspet Gillespie! Every face a commentary on the "rights of man" —every little head crowned with a three-footed stool, its "cap of liberty." There they go,—a living forest, less leafy, less orderly than the Birnam wood that moved to Dunsinane. Thus should it be— this left a tyrant—that sought one. But the day of days, in Elspet Gillespie's ragamuffin college, was *Candlemas day*. Then the very madness of young mirth prevailed, washing off the jagged recollections of bygone sufferings, and sweetening down the three hundred and sixty-four sorrows of the season. Elspet on that day wore a smile on her face, and a high *caul* cap on her head—the *taurds* and cat invisible—locked up, it may be, in passive unity—the envied brute and detested leather. No matter how wrapped our vulgar days, Candlemas claimed a clean *sark* to every laddie—to every lassie a white frock, and to each a white pocket napkin. A king and queen were, by the breath of Elspet, created on the spot. Who

Bawbee, *a halfpenny.* Laigh, *lowly.* Skailing, *going out.*
Caul, *triangular shape.* Sark, *shirt.*

E'en the stout stems of summer full often must quail
To this rattling, brattling, head-breaking hail.
I'll not say a word of how rudely she breaks
On the dream of the garret-doomed maid, and awakes
A thousand regrets in the marrowless lass,
And cruelly mimics the "touch on the glass,"

Marrowless, *unmarried.*

---

the distinguished? It was the undeviating custom for parents to tender, on Candlemas eve, a guerdon to our tutoress, less or lesser, as earthly means permitted. So it fell out somehow that, in every rememberable instance, either the baker or the butcher rejoiced in the royal issue. Hence our gossiping mothers of meaner note did, in their envy, whisper that Eppie's royal rule was, "Wha buys the whistle?" Never mind that, we've seen the like since then—no disparagement to "the powers that breathe." Two teaspoonfuls of sweeties and an orange was laid on every happy hand. The fiddler comes—all on foot at once—all at once in motion—twenty white napkins flutter over twenty pretty heads. Fiddler! what care they for a fiddler? They *see* the fiddle! The dance started when he began to tune—the dance continues—he is tuning still—hands up! Patter, patter, patter—forty little feet pattering! Think of that when you see the hail dance to the *whirr* of a May shower! Oh! the days of childhood! Voyage thereafter as we may, on smooth or on broken water, these are the landmarks that will never fade. The blue of our native hills may be lost to the eye for long, long years, yet once again we press their heathy belts; but you, ye sunny scenes of infancy, though ye glimmer through every darkness, and at every distance, we meet never again. "Old Father Frost" was the result of a sportive contest in rhyming between the author and Mr. Adam, whose verses are subjoined, as well for their native prettiness as their giving interest and character to the whole.

    Old Father Frost hath children twain,
    Begotten 'twixt him and his Lady Rain;
    Though he is harsh, yet mild is she,
    And this is seen in their family.
     Old Father Frost and his family!

With her cold little pearls, that dance, bound, and
    play,
Like our ain bonnie bairns on Candlemas day.
You know her meek sister? Oh, soft is the fall
Of *her* fairy footsteps on hut and on hall!
To hide the old father's bleak doings below,
In pity she cometh, the minist'ring snow.

    Ain, *own*.   Bairns, *children*.   Bonnie, *pretty*.

Yes, Father Frost is a hard old churl,
On his upper lip there's a bitter curl;
And his black ill-favoured visage throws
A sombre shade o'er his pale blue nose.
    Old Father Frost and his family!

When the summer heat hath passed away,
And gentle Rain gives up her sway,
Old Father Frost, with his iron hand,
Seizes and binds each northern land.
    Old Father Frost and his family!

And hard it were for the creatures of earth,
Were it not that Lady Rain gives birth
To her chaste and kindly daughter, Snow,
Who throws her mantle o'er all below.
    Old Father Frost and his family!

For stern is the fiat of Father Frost,
He chains the waters though tempest tos't;
And he freezes up the very ground
Till it yields a ringing metal sound.
    Old Father Frost and his family!

But like the Paynim maid in the minstrel tale,
Who released the knight from her father's jail,
Sweet sister Snow sets prisoners free,
And mitigates Frost's severity.
    Old Father Frost and his family!

With her mantle she covers the shelterless trees,
As they groan to the howl of the Borean breeze;
And baffles the search of the subtle wind,
Guarding each crevice lest it should find
Its moaning way to the fireless fold
Of the trembling young and the weeping old,
When through her white bosom the daisy appears,
She greets the fair stranger with motherly tears!
And they mingle so sweet with the golden ray
Of the struggling beam that chides her away.
But where's the last speck of her brightness seen,
Mid the bursting spring and its saucy green?
In the coldest side of yon lone churchyard,
Neglected graves she loveth to ward;
But not where gorgeous marble pleads,
And frequent foot of mourner treads;
But down by the stranger's noteless lair,
Where sighs are few and footsteps rare,
She loveth, she loveth to linger there!
O'er hearts forgotten that sleep below,
There is none to weep but the friendly snow.

Fold, *shelter*.

Not so kind by half is brother Hail,
Who rattles about in his coat of mail,
And bends and shatters both shrub and flower,
In the wanton display of his father's power.
    Old Father Frost and his family!

But Frost, and Rain, and Hail, and Snow,
Come at your time when you come below;
And we'll welcome you all with a cheerful smile,
And drink and laugh and sing the while.
    Old Father Frost and his family!

AUTUMN WINDS.

Air—" Bonnie House o' Airly."

Oh, ye waesome winds, hoo your mourning grieves,
    Hoo your sighing an' moaning fear me!
As ye toss an' tear the trembling leaves
    That ye cherished when *he* was near me.

I've kent ye woo them—I've heard ye woo,
    As saftly as woman's lane sighing;
When ye slyly kissed the cozie dew
    Frae their faulded bosoms lying.

Now nightly athwart the naked plain,
    Ye are whirling the saucy snaw in;
Ye've changed the dew to the pelting rain,
    Till your poor droukit leaves are fa'in.

Hae ye fausely strayed 'mang misty groves,
    Wi' ice-wreathed maidens to marrow?
Oh, they've come an' slain your bonnie summer loves,
    An' driven ye daft wi' sorrow!

Cozie, *snug.*
Daft, *mad.*
Droukit, *drenched.*
Faulded, *folded.*
Fausely, *falsely.*
Frae, *from.*
Hae, *have.*
Hoo, *how.*
Kent, *known.*
Lane, *lone.*
Marrow, *keep company with.*
Saftly, *softly.*
Waesome, *woesome.*

But *my* love is true, ye winds that blaw,
    And your fauseness maunna fear me;
His kind heart never will flit nor fa',
    Nor own anither dearie.

There's ae green branch on yon blighted tree,
    An' the lave a' darkly dwining;
There's ae bricht e'e looks love to me,
    Like the weird licht o'er me shining.

Yet oh, ye winds, hoo your wailing grieves!
    Hoo your sighing an' moaning fear me!
As ye toss an' tear the dowie grey leaves
    That waur green, green, when he was near me.

Blaw, *blow.*
Bricht, *bright.*
Dowie, *sickly.*
Dwining, *withering.*
Fauseness, *falsely.*
Flit, *to remove.*
Hoo, *how.*
Lave, *rest.*
Maunna, *must not.*
Waur, *were.*
Weird licht, *light of my destiny.*

OH, MARY! WHEN YOU THINK OF ME.

[For a period of seventeen years, I was employed in a great weaving factory in Aberdeen. It contained upwards of three hundred looms, worked by as many male and female weavers. 'T was a sad place, indeed, and many a curiosity sort of man and woman entered that blue gate. Amongst the rest, that little, sly fellow Cupid would steal past "Willie, the porter" (who never dreamed of such a being)—steal in amongst us, and make a very harvest of it. Upon the remembrance of one of his rather graver doings, the song of "Mary" is composed. One of our shopmates, a virtuous young woman, fairly, though unconsciously, carried away the whole bulk and value of a poor weaver's heart. He became restless and miserable, but could never muster spirit to speak his flame. "*He* never told his love"—yes, he told it to me. At his request, I told it to Mary, and she laughed. Five weeks passed away, and I saw him to the churchyard. For many days ere he died, Mary watched by his bedside, a sorrowful woman, indeed. Never did widow's tears fall more burningly. It is twenty years since then. She is now a wife and a mother; but the remembrance of that, their last meeting, still haunts her sensitive nature, as if she had done a deed of blood.]

Oh, Mary! when you think of me,
 Let pity hae its share, love;
Tho' others mock my misery,
 Do you in mercy spare, love.

Hae, *have.*

OH, MARY! WHEN YOU THINK OF ME.

My heart, oh, Mary! own'd but thee,
And sought for thine so fervently;
The saddest tear e'er wet my e'e,
Ye ken *wha* brocht it there, love.

Oh, lookna wi' that witching look,
  That wiled my peace awa', love!
An' dinna let me hear you sigh,
  It tears my heart in twa, love!
    Resume the frown ye wont to wear,
    Nor shed the unavailing tear,
    The hour of doom is drawing near,
    An' welcome be its ca', love!

How could ye hide a thought sae kind,
  Beneath sae cauld a brow, love?
The broken heart it winna bind
  Wi' gowden bandage now, love.
    No, Mary! mark yon reckless shower!
    It hung aloof in scorching hour,
    An' helps nae now the feckless flower
    That sinks beneath its flow, love.

Brocht, *brought.*
Ca', *call.*
Cauld, *cold.*
Dinna, *do not.*

Feckless, *feeble.*
Ken, *know.*
Lookna, *look not.*
Nae, *not.*

Sae, *so.*
Twa, *twain.*
Wha, *who.*
Winna, *will not.*

I'VE SOUGHT IN LANDS AYONT THE SEA.

Written at Stocks, near Tring, 1841.

Air—" My Normandie."

I 'VE sought in lands ayont the sea
A hame—a couthie hame for thee,
An' honeysickle bursts around
The blithesome hame that I hae found;
Then dinna grudge your heather bell—
Oh, fretna for your flowerless fell—
Here dale an' down mair fair to see,
Than ought in our ain bleak countrie!

Come o'er the waters, dinna fear,
The lav'rock lilts as lo'esome here,
An' mony a sweet, around, above,
Shall welcome o'er my Jessie, love.

Ain, *own.*
Ayont, *beyond.*
Couthie, *comfortable.*
Dinna, *do not.*
Fretna, *fret not.*
Hame, *home.*
Lav'rock, *lark.*
Lilts, *sings.*
Lo'esome, *lovely.*
Mair, *more.*

My hame wi' halesome gear is fu',
My heart wi' loweing love for you;
Oh, haste, my Jessie, come an' see
The hame—the heart that waits for thee!

But mind ye, lass, the fleetfu' hours,
They wait nae—spare nae fouk nor flowers,
An' sair are fouk and flowers to blame,
Wha wishfu', wastefu' wait for them.
Oh, bide nae lang in swither, then,
Since flowers an' fouk may wither, then;
But come, as lang 's I hae to gie
A hame—a heart to welcome thee!

Fleetfu', *fleeting.*   Hae, *have.*   Nae, *not.*
Fouk, *folk.*   Halesome, *wholesome.*   Sair, *much.*
Gear, *furniture.*   Loweing, *burning.*   Swither, *doubt.*

I WOULDNA—OH! I COULDNA LOOK.

"Should auld acquaintance be forgot?" Ay, faith; and in some cases the sooner the better too.

I WOULDNA—oh! I couldna look
   On that sweet face again;
I daurna trust my simple heart,
   Now it's ance mair my ain.

I wouldna thole what I hae thol'd,
   Sic dule I wouldna dree,
For a' that love could now unfold
   Frae woman's witchfu' e'e.

I've mourn'd until the waesome moon
   Has sunk ahint the hill,
An' seen ilk sparkling licht aboon
   Creep o'er me, mournin' still.

Aboon, *above*.	Dule, *sorrow*.	Mair, *more*.
Ahint, *behind*.	Frae, *from*.	Sic, *such*.
Ance, *once*.	Hae, *have*.	Thole, *endure*.
Daurna, *durst not*.	Ilk, *each*.	Waesome, *woesome*.
Dree, *undergo*.	Licht, *light*.	Wouldna, *would not*.

I've thocht my very mither's hame
    Was hameless-like to me;
Nor could I think this warld the same
    That I was wont to see.

But years o' mingled care hae past,
    Wi' blinks o' joy between;
An' yon heart-hoarded form at last
    Forsakes my doited een.

Sae cauld and dark my bosom now,
    Sic hopes lie buried there!
That sepulchre whaur love's saft lowe
    May never kindle mair.

I couldna trust this foolish heart
    When its ance mair my ain;
I couldna—oh! I daurna look
    On Mary's face again!

Ain, *own*.
Ance, *once*.
Couldna, *could not*.
Daurna, *durst not*.
Doited, *confused*.
Een, *eyes*.
Hae, *have*.
Lowe, *flame*.
Mair, *more*.
Sae, *so*.
Sic, *such*.
Thocht, *thought*.

JEANIE'S GRAVE.

I saw my true Love first on the banks of queenly Tay,
Nor did I deem it yielding my trembling heart away;
I feasted on her deep dark eye, and loved it more and more,
For, oh! I thought I ne'er had seen a look so kind before!

I heard my true Love sing, and she taught me many a strain,
But a voice so sweet, oh! never shall my cold ear hear again,
In all our friendless wanderings, in homeless penury,
Her gentle song and jetty eye were all unchanged to me.

I saw my true Love fade—I heard her latest sigh—
I wept no frivolous weeping when I closed her lightless eye;
Far from her native Tay she sleeps, and other waters lave
The markless spot where Ury creeps around my Jeanie's grave.

Move noiseless, gentle Ury! around my Jeanie's bed,
And I'll love thee, gentle Ury! where'er my footsteps tread;

For sooner shall thy fairy wave return from yonder sea,
Than I forget yon lowly grave, and all it hides from me.*

---

* Three mountain streamlets brawl separately down their breakneck journey, and tumble in peace together at the woods at Newton, near Old Rayne. This quiet confluence is the Ury. Like worn-out racers, these boisterous burns take breath, gliding along in harmonious languor some three or four miles, when the peaceful Ury is, as it were, cut through by the Gadie, a desperately crabbed-looking rivulet, raging and rumbling from Benachie. From this last annoyance, Ury moves onward in noiseless sweetness, winding and winding, as if aware of its own brief course, and all unwilling to leave the braes that hap the heroes of Harlaw. By-and-by, it creeps mournfully past the sequestered graveyard of Inverury, kisses the "Bass," and is swallowed up in the blue waters of the Don; its whole extent being only ten miles. Close by the graveyard stands the Bass of Inverury—a conical-shaped hill, thickly studded with trees. The gloomy legends told of its origin and subsequent uses, would make one readily own its fitting neighbourhood to a place of skulls. One will tell you that, once upon a time, the plague came upon Scotland, and Inverury had its share; that a deserted house stood then on the banks of the Ury—thither was carried the infected till the number of patients outran the skill and resources of their friends, who assembled to deliberate on "ways and means." It was then settled upon, that, to shorten present suffering, and to secure future safety, the best way was to bury them forthwith, house and all. It was done then. Hence the "Bass." "Some maintain that the Bass has been used for judicial purposes. By others it is supposed to be of a sepulchral character; and to contain the remains of Eth or Aoth, a Pictish king, who was killed a year after his accession in A.D. 881 The old rhyme of Thomas the Rhymer,

' When Dee and Don shall run in one,
　And Tweed shall run in Tay,
　　The bonnie water of Ury
　　　Shall bear the Bass away,'

is in every one's mouth in this district."

At Newton are some remarkable lofty stones (monoliths). The Antiquarian Society have had casts made of the inscriptions and figures on them, but they have hitherto defied the attempts of the learned to decypher them.

THEY SPEAK O' WYLES.

AIR—"Gin a bodie meet a bodie."

They speak o' wyles in woman's smiles,
   An' ruin in her e'e—
I ken they bring a pang at whiles
   That's unco sair to dree;
But mind ye this, the half-ta'en kiss,
   The first fond fa'in' tear,
Is, Heaven kens, fu' sweet amends
   An' tints o' heaven here.

When twa leal hearts in fondness meet,
   Life's tempests howl in vain—
The very tears o' love are sweet
   When paid with tears again.
Shall sapless prudence shake its pow,
   Shall cauldrife caution fear?
Oh, dinna, dinna droun the lowe
   That lichts a heaven here!

Cauldrife, *coldish*.   Ken, *know*.   Sair, *sore*.
Dinna, *do not*.   Leal, *true*.   Unco, *very*.
Dree, *endure*.   Lichts, *lights*.   Wyles, *cunning*.
Droun, *drown*.   Lowe, *flame*.

THE LAST TRYST.

This nicht ye 'll cross the bosky glen,
Ance mair, oh, would ye meet me then?
I 'll seem as bygane bliss an' pain
                Were a' forgot.

I winna weep to weary thee,
Nor seek the love ye canna gie;—
Whaur first we met, oh, let that be
                The parting spot!

The hour just when the faithless licht
O' yon pale star forsakes the nicht;
I wouldna pain ye wi' the blicht
                Ye 've brought to me.

Nor would I that yon proud cauld ray
Should mock me wi' its scornfu' play;—
The sunken een and tresses gray
                Ye maunna see.

Ance, *once.*
Blicht, *blight.*
Bosky, *wild, unfrequented.*
Bygane, *bygone.*
Canna, *cannot.*
Cauld, *cold.*
Een, *eyes.*
Gie, *give.*
Licht, *light.*
Mair, *more.*
Maunna, *must not.*
Nicht, *night.*
Whaur, *where.*
Winna, *will not.*

Wi' sindered hearts few words will sair,
An' brain-dried grief nae tears can spare;
These bluidless lips shall never mair
                Name thine or thee.

At murky nicht, oh, meet me then!
Restore my plighted troth again;
Your bonnie bride shall never ken
                Your wrangs to me.

Bluidless, *bloodless*.   Nicht, *night*.   Sair, *satisfy*.
Ken, *know*.   Mair, *more*.   Sindered, *parted*.
Nae, *no*.   Murky, *dark*.   Wrangs, *wrongs*.

ONE OF THE HEART'S STRUGGLES.

AIR—"Willie was a wanton wag."

"Oh! let me gang, ye dinna ken
   How sair my mither flate yestreen—
An', mournin' o'er and o'er again,
   Speir'd whaur I gaed sae late at e'en.
An' aye I saw her dicht her een—
   My very heart maist brak to see 't—
I'd byde a flyte though e'er sae keen,
   But canna, canna thole her greet."

"Oh! blessin's guard my lassie's brow,
   And fend her couthie heart frae care;
Her lowein' breast o' love sae fu'—
   How can I grudge a mither's share?

Brak, *broke.*
Byde, *endure.*
Canna, *cannot.*
Couthie, *kind.*
Dicht, *wipe.*
Dinna, *do not.*
Een, *eyes.*
Fend, *protect.*
Flate, *cried.*
Flyte, *scolding.*
Gaed, *went.*
Gang, *go.*
Greet, *tear-shedding.*
Ken, *know.*
Lowein', *burning.*
Maist, *almost.*
Sae, *so.*
Sair, *much.*
Speir'd, *asked.*
Thole, *endure.*
Whaur, *where.*
Yestreen, *last night.*

The hinnysuckle 's no sae fair,
 In gloamin's dewy pearl weet,
As my love's e'e when tremblin' there
 The tear that owns a mither's greet.

" A heart a' warmed to mither's love—
 Oh! that 's the heart whaur I wad be;
An' when a mither's lips reprove,
 Oh! gie me then the glist'nin' e'e.
For feckless fa's that look on me,
 Howe'er sae feigned in cunnin's sweet—
And loveless—luckless—is the e'e
 That, tearless, kens a mither greet."

Feckless, *feebly*.
Gie, *give*.
Gloamin', *twilight*.
Greet, *tears*.

Greet, *cry*.
Kens, *knows*.
Sae, *so*.

Wad, *would*.
Weet, *wet*.
Whaur, *where*.

YE DINNA KEN YON BOWER.

Air—"Jenny Nettles."

Ye dinna ken yon bower,
Frae the glow'rin' warl' hidden,
Ye maunna ken yon bower
   Bonnie in the gloamin'.
Nae woodbine sheds a fragrance there,
Nae rose, nae daffodillie fair;
But, oh! yon flow'r beyond compare
   That blossoms in the gloamin'.

There's little licht in yon bower,
Day and darkness elbow ither,
That's the licht in yon bower,
   Bonnie in the gloamin'.
Awa' ye sun, wi' lavish licht,
And bid brown Benachie guid nicht;
To me a star mair dearly bricht
   Aye glimmers in the gloamin'.

Bonnie, *beautiful*.
Bricht, *bright*.
Dinna, *do not*.
Frae, *from*.
Gloamin', *after twilight*.
Glow'rin', *staring*.
Guid, *good*.
Hidden, *hiding*.
Ither, *each other*.
Ken, *know*.
Licht, *light*.
Mair, *more*.
Maunna, *must not*.
Nae, *no*.
Nicht, *night*.
Warl', *world*.

There's nae a sound in yon bower,
Merl's sough nor mavis singin';
Whispers saft in yon bower,
  Mingle in the gloamin'.
What though drowsie lav'rocks rest,
Cow'rin' in their sangless nest?
When, oh! the voice that I like best
  Cheers me in the gloamin'.

There's artless truth in yon bower,
Sweeter than the scented blossom;
Bindin' hearts in yon bower,
  Glowin' in the gloamin'.
The freshness o' the upland lea,
The fragrance o' the blossom'd pea,
A' mingle in her breath to me,
  Sichin' in the gloamin'.

CONCLUDING CHORUS.

Then haud awa' frae yon bower,
Cauldrife breast or loveless bosom;
True love dwells in yon bower,
  Gladdest in the gloamin'.

Awa', *away*.   Lav'rocks, *larks*.   Sangless, *songless*.
Cauldrife, *coldish*.   Nae, *not*.   Siching, *sighing*.
Frae, *from*.   Saft, *soft*.   Sough, *sound*.
Haud, *keep*.

BONNIE MAY.

AIR—"The year that's awa'."

Oh, whaur hae ye gane, bonnie May
    Hae ye left us for ever an' aye?
Your daft brither, June, brak in wi' a stoun',
    Maist frichtit our birdies away,
            Oh, May!
An' feint a bit liltie hae they.

Our gowans droop wither'd an' grey,
    Our bairnies creep sullen an' blae;
Through blifferts o' caul' they yaumer an' yaul,
    An' want ye to warm them, May,
            Oh, May!
Our dear, duddie bairnies, May.

Blae, *blue, cold.*
Blifferts, *gusts.*
Brak, *broke.*
Brither, *brother.*
Caul', *cold.*
Daft, *mad.*
Duddie, *ragged.*
Feint, *deuce.*
Frichtit, *frighted.*
Gane, *gone.*
Gowans, *field daisies.*
Hae, *have.*
Liltie, *song.*
Maist, *almost.*
Stoun, *fury.*
Whaur, *where.*
Yaumer an' yaul, *weeping and howling.*

BONNIE MAY.

The whir o' the witherin' wind
  Drives madly o'er burn an' brae;
The tremblin' breird fa's sadden an' sear'd,
  An' kens nae the nicht frae the day,
          Oh, May!
An' hae ye forsaken us, May?

Our crafters look crabbit an' fey,
  Our wee bits o' bushes decay;
They crouch in the yard, cauld blabs on ilk beard,
  An' greet to the mornin' grey,
          Oh, May!
They miss the lythe licht o' their May.

I've nae mair to sing or to say,
  But come, gin you're comin', sweet May,
Ere Martinmas drear, set the Factor asteer,
  An' then there's the deevil to pay,
          Oh, May!
Our stools an' our tubbies away!

Asteer, *abroad.*
Blabs, *blobs.*
Breird, *braird.**
Brae, *hill.*
Burn, *brook.*
Cauld, *cold.*
Crafters, *crofters, small tenants.*
Fey, *foredoomed.*
Factor, *agent.*
Gin, *if.*
Greet, *weep.*
Hae, *have.*
Ilk, *each.*
Kens nae, *knows not.*
Licht, *light.*
Lythe, *warm.*
Nae mair, *no more.*
Tubbies, *tubs distrained for rent.*
Wee, *little.*
Whir, *rush.*

* "Braird," the first shootings of the crop.

LINES WRITTEN AT RAVENSCRAIG,

A RUIN ON THE BANKS OF UGIE, NEAR PETERHEAD, ABERDEENSHIRE.

> "A building—such a one
> As age to age might add for uses vile,
> A windowless, deformed, and dreary pile."
> SHELLEY.

Yon 's Ravenscraig, wi' riven ha',
A thousand winters shook its wa'—
Tired Time let scythe an' san'glass fa',
    To breathe awhile at Ugie.

For here, by brake, by burn an' lea,
Fair Nature freaks sae changefullie!
Now lauchin' daft, syne greets to see
    Yon grim, grey towers at Ugie.

An' wha can mark yon dungeon dour,
Unmindfu' o' the waesome hour,
When man o'er man, wi' fiendish power,
    Made sick the tremblin' Ugie.

Daft, *madly*.   Ha', *hall*.   Syne, *then*.
Dour, *surly*.   San'glass, *hour-glass*.   Waesome, *woeful*.
Greets, *weeps*.

Bring ivy wi' its peacefu' green,
Gae hide ilk hoar, unhallow'd stane;
They maunna bloat yon bonnie een
    That watch the gushin' Ugie.

For yonder 's she, in love's loved dress,
In youth, in truth, in tenderness—
Sure Heaven lent that bonnie face
    To bless the tearfu' Ugie!

'T is sic a face, 't is sic a mien,
An' oh! sic wylie, witchin' een,
Gars Time upon his elbow lean,
    An' sich to cross the Ugie.

Bonnie, *lovely*.
Een, *eyes*.
Gars, *causeth*.
Ilk, *each*.
Maunna, *must not*.
Sic, *such like*.
Sich, *sigh*.
Wylie, *sly*.

A LETTER TO THE EDITOR OF THE ———.

Inverury, March 1st, 1844.

Sir,—In your paper, the other week, I read of a woman, Cameron, Overgate, Dundee, found dead—her child, a boy of seven years, sleeping beside her. She expired unknown to any—she and her little son lying on a *shakedown* in a wretched hovel—not a morsel of food, but every mark of starvation, cold, and hunger. Now, sir, having myself tasted the bitter cup—having seen death at work in this same hideous form—the above tragedy affected me very much. I do not think ill of mankind, but the contrary. I would not reflect on the *goodwill* of those who *undertake*, and whose duty it then *is*, to watch the abodes of misery. Reproach may not apply to the *will* of parties so placed; but what could the mildest say of that blameable and fatal *ignorance* that thus defeats the very best ends of mercy—leaving a human creature to struggle with death in its most revolting attitude—then mock the whole with a sort of posthumous wail? I sincerely believe that there was not one in Dundee, that night—whether on hardest pallet or softest down—but would have started in the dark hour, ministered to yon perishing woman, soothed the little trembler at her cold breast, and been happy. But who knew of it? Why, everybody, *next* day, when the *white coffin** is seen borne along by a troop of pale-faced *existences*, whose present suffering

---

* In Dundee, it lately was the case, if not still, that paupers' coffins were not allowed to be blackened.

is nowise smoothed by the prospect offered in their then *dowie* occupation, and the fate that may be their own one cold dark night, ere long. Starvation to death is not uncommon amongst us; yet we are in the nineteenth century—the pearl age of benevolent societies, charity-schools, and "useful knowledge." Would benevolence be perverted, charity made colder, or the knowledge *useless*, that made us timeously acquainted with catastrophes like these? In Aberdeen, the other week, an aged man was found dead in his garret, with every appearance of want and wretchedness? How came it to be known? Did the elder of the district discover it while on his round of Christian inquiry? Did some benevolent ruler in a benevolent society miss his poor old neighbour? Weeks and weeks his tottering footsteps had not been seen on the pavement, or heard in his naked abode. He is dead—starved dead,—and the stench of his half-consumed body first gives notice, that "however man may act by man, Death is at his post." Oh, that some kind-hearted creature, with a turn for statistical computation, would lend me a hand! It might be made clear, I think, that in a population of sixty thousand, one hundred could be spared (by regular changes) to hunt Misery to its very heels, and scare it, at least, from its more hideous feasts. Say that districts are divided into wards, each ward having its appointed inspector, whose duty it should be to observe *earnestly*, and report *faithfully*, all concerning the poverty-stricken residents in his charge.

That the "Murder of Neglect" is perpetrated in this land is one terrible fact, and it is as true, though, alas! not so terrifying, that he who is ignorant of it, or, knowing it, feels it only as an incident per course, bestowing upon it a *fusionless* shrug, and a " woes me,"—*that man has blood upon his head!* We are the children of one Father, travelling together on the broad and brief way to eternity. Alas! for such unequal equipment—seeing we must at last pull up at the one same stage! You will forgive me all this preaching, but my soul is in it, and last night I composed the following lines bearing that way. If you think these, or any sentiments here expressed, would, if made public, in any way move an additional feeling in favour of the "Overgate Orphan," I would be proud and happy.

THE OVERGATE ORPHAN.

'Tis the lone wail of woman, a mother's last woe,
And tearless the eye when the soul weepeth so—
Nor fuel nor food in yon windowless lair,
The sleeping is watched by the dying one there.

"Oh, wauken nae, wauken nae, my dowie dear!
My dead look would wither your wee heart wi' fear;
Sleep on till yon cauld moon is set in the sea,
Gin mornin', hoo cauld will your wauk'nin' be!

"Ye creep to a breast, Jamie, cauld as the snaw,
Ye hang roun' a heart, Jamie, sinkin' awa';
I'm laith, laith to leave ye, though fain would I dee
Gin Heaven would lat my lost laddie wi' me!"

Awaken, lone trembler, the moon has no light,
And the grey glint of morning drives back the fell night;
Her last look is fixing in yon frozen tear—
Awaken, lone trembler, thy home is not here!

The death-grasp awoke him—the struggle is o'er,
He moans to the ear that will listen no more:
"You're caulder than me, mither, cauld though I be,
And *that* look is nae like your ain look to me.

Ain, *own*.
Cauld, *cold*.
Caulder, *colder*.
Dee, *die*.
Dowie, *sickly*.

Gin, *by*.
Gin, *if*.
Hoo, *how*.
Lair, *dwelling*.
Laith, *loth*.

Lat, *let*.
Nae, *not*.
Wauken, *waken*.
Wauk'nin', *wakening*.

"I dreamt how my father came back frae the deid,
An' waesome an' eerie the looks that he gied;
He wyled ye awa' till ye sindered frae me—
Oh, hap me, my mither, I'm cauld—like to dee!"·

The creaking white coffin is hurried away,
The mourners all motley, and shrivelled, and gray;
Each meagre one muttering it over yon bier,—
"So colder my home is—oh, God! it were here!"

Deid, *dead*.	Gied, *gave*.	Sindered, *separated*.
Eerie, *wild*.	Hap, *cover*.	Wyled, *cozened*.
Frae, *from*.	Shrivelled, *shrunken*.	

YTHANSIDE.

I HAD ae nicht, and only ane,
    On flow'ry Ythanside,
An' kith or kindred I hae nane
    That dwall by Ythanside;
Yet midnicht dream and morning vow
    At hame they winna bide,
But pu', and pu' my willing heart
    Awa' to Ythanside.

What gars ilk restless, wand'ring wish
    Seek aye to Ythanside,
An' hover round yon fairy bush
    That spreads o'er Ythanside?
I think I see its pawkie boughs,
    Whaur lovers weel might hide;
An' oh! what heart could safely sit
    Yon nicht at Ythanside?

Bide, *stay*.
Dwall, *dwell*.
Gars, *causeth*.
Ilk, *every*.

Nicht, *night*.
Pawkie, *sly*.
Pu', *pull*.

Weel, *well*.
Whaur, *where*.
Winna, *will not*.

Could I return and own the scaith
 I thole frae Ythanside,
Would her mild e'e bend lythe on me
 Ance mair on Ythanside?
Or, would she crush my lowly love
 Beneath a brow o' pride?
I daurna claim, and maunna blame,
 Her heart on Ythanside.

I'll rue yon high and heathy seat*
 That hangs o'er Ythanside;
I'll rue the mill whaur burnies meet;
 I'll rue ye, Ythanside.

Ance, *once*.	Frae, *from*.	Maunna, *must not*.
Daurna, *dare not*.	Lythe, *kindly*.	Scaith, *hurt*.
E'e, *eye*.	Mair, *more*.	Thole, *endure*.

---

* In the woods of Essilmont, there is a most romantic looking pinnacle overhanging the water Ythan. Nature has scooped in it a beautiful little gallery. There the late Miss Gordon, of Essilmont (an old castle, the seat of the Cheynes of Essilmont, was daily seen surrounded by the children of the neighbouring peasantry, teaching them all things needful to their situation in life—their duty to God and the world.

Ythan rises in Forgue, out of Fondland Hill, from two springs; is about 15 miles long, without reckoning its windings; and has six ferry boats; is deep and black, and hence dangerous. Yet it abounds with pearls, which, were they waited for till they became ripe, would turn to good account. Hence one of our poets (Hawthornden, in an epitaph on a nobleman buried here), addressing himself to this river in a melancholy strain, hath said,

  "Ythan! thy pearly coronet let fall."

The top-pearl in the crown of Scotland, is reported to have been found in Kelly, a little brook that falls into Ythan in Methlick parish.

An' you, ye Moon, wi' luckless licht,
    Pour'd a' your gowden tide
O'er sic a brow!—sic een, yon nicht!—
    Oh, weary Ythanside!

    Licht, *light*.   Sic, *such*.

Sir Thomas Menzies of Cults having procured it—for beauty and bigness, the best at any time found in Scotland,—and having found, by the judgment of the best jewellers in Edinburgh, that it was most precious, and of a very high value, went up to London and gifted it to the king,—this was in the year 1620,—who, in retribution, gave him 12 or 14 chalders of victual about Dumfermling, and the custom of merchant-goods in Aberdeen during his life.

In the reign of King Charles I., the trade was considered of sufficient moment to be worthy the attention of the Parliament. The pearls of Scotland long shared with those of Bohemia the reputation of being the best found in Europe, though they were held to be very far inferior to those of the East.—[Description of the Diocese of Aberdeen, and Notes to it; presented to the Spalding Club by the Earl of Aberdeen.]

A CHIEFTAIN UNKNOWN TO THE QUEEN.
1843.

Auld Scotland cried " Welcome your Queen !"
   Ilk glen echoed " Welcome your Queen !"
While turret and tower to mountain and moor,
   Cried " Wauken and welcome our Queen !"

Syne, oh ! sic deray was exprest,
   As Scotland for lang hadna seen ;
When bodies cam bickerin' a' clad in their best—
   To beck to their bonnie young Queen.

When a' kinds o' colours cam south,
   An' scarlet* frae sly Aberdeen :
Ilk flutterin' heart flitted up to the mouth,
   A' pantin' to peep at our Queen.

There were Earls on that glittering strand,
   Wi' diamonded Dame mony ane ;
An' weel might it *seem* that the happiest land
   Was trod by the happiest Queen.

A', *every*.   Beck, *bow*.   Sic, *such*.
Bickerin', *a fighting run*.   Deray, *noisy gladness*.   Syne, *then*.
   Ilk, *every*.   Wauken, *awaken*.

* Scarlet is the town's livery.

Then mony a chieftain's heart
  Beat high 'neath its proud tartan screen;
But one sullen chief stood afar and apart,
  Nor recked he the smile o' a Queen.

" Wha 's he winna blink on our Queen,
  Wi' his haffets sae lyart and lean?"
O ho! it is Want, wi' his gathering gaunt,
  An' his million of mourners unseen.

Proud Scotland cried "Hide them; oh, hide!*
  An' lat nae them licht on her een;
Wi' their bairnies bare, it would sorrow her sair!
  For a mither's heart moves in our Queen."

Bairnies, *infants*.	Licht, *fall*.	On her een, *in her sight*.
Blink, *look*.	Lyart, *haggard*.	
Haffets, *cheeks*.		Sae, *so*.

---

* The Paisley weavers formed a portion in the retinue of this sulky chief. At the very time Scotland, with its best foot foremost, was prancing before its beloved Sovereign, the street orange-sellers of Edinburgh were ordered " to bed" till the Queen left, by the same sage authorities that were snoring when the Queen came. So—so—behind the fairest painting you will find mere *canvas*—aye, canvas!

THE DRUNKARD'S DREAM.

"Who hath woe? Who hath sorrows? They that tarry long at the wine."
Proverbs xxiii. 29, 30.

Oh, tempt me not to the drunkard's draught,
   With its soul-consuming gleam!
Oh, hide me from the woes that waft
   Around the drunkard's dream!

When night in holy silence brings
   The God-willed hour of sleep,
Then, then the red-eyed revel swings
   Its bowl of poison deep!

When morning waves its golden hair,
   And smiles o'er hill and lea,
One sick'ning ray is doomed to glare
   On yon rude revelry!

The rocket's flary moment sped,
   Sinks black'ning back to earth;
Yet darker—deeper sinks his head
   Who shares the drunkard's mirth!

Know ye the sleep the drunkard knows?
   That sleep, oh, who may tell?
Or who can speak the fiendful throes
   Of his self-heated hell?

The soul all reft of heav'nly mark—
   Defaced God's image there—
Rolls down and down yon abyss dark,
   Thy howling home, Despair!

Or bedded his head on broken hearts,
   Where slimy reptiles creep;
And the ball-less eye of Death still darts
   Black fire on the drunkard's sleep!

And lo! their coffin'd bosoms rife,
   That bled in his ruin wild!
The cold, cold lips of his shrouded wife,
   Press lips of his shrouded child!

So fast—so deep the hold they keep!
   Hark! that unhallow'd scream;
Guard us, oh God! from the drunkard's sleep—
   From the drunkard's demon-dream!

CAN YE FORGET?

> " My sight
> Is dim to see that charactered in vain
> On this unfeeling leaf, which burns the brain
> And eats into it, blotting all things fair
> And wise and good, which time had written there."
> SHELLEY.

Can ye forget yon sunny day
   Whan sparkling Ury murmured by?
Whaur birdies in their blythest way
   Poured April sangs athwart the sky?
How little, little then kent I
   Sae fause the lip that prest to mine;
Oh! wha could think yon fever'd sigh
   Cam frae a breast sae cauld as thine?

But weel mind I as o'er my head
   A wee, wee lanesome birdie sang;
Sae waesome did its music plead,
   I scarce could hide the tear it brang.

Blythest, *gladdest*.   Fause, *false*.   Waesome, *mournfully*.
Brang, *brought*.   Kent, *knew*.   Wee, *little*.
Cauld, *cold*.   Sae, *so*.   Weel, *well*.

My heart maist frae my bosom sprang,
   Syne trembling sank wi' bodefu' knell,
For, oh! I feared that I ere lang
   Micht maen in siclike lonely wail.

Sinsyne I 've kent cauld gloamin' come,
   Whan blae and wae the Ury ran;
Whan cow'rin' birds a' nestled dumb,
   An' cheerless nicht lower'd o'er the lawn.
Sic time my bursting bosom faun'
   The slack'ning gush that nane micht see;
And aye the licht's unlo'esome dawn
   Brang life an' love to a' but me!

I had nae hinnied words to woo,
   Nae gainfu' gifts had I to spare;
But, oh! I had a heart sae true,
   That nocht could shift, that nane should share.
Ae trembling wish alane lived there—
   Ae hope that held the witless way;
That hope is gane, an' evermair
   Left darkness owre life's dowie day.

Ae, *one*.
Blae, *blue*.
Brang, *brought*.
Cauld, *cold*.
Dowie, *gloomy*.
Faun', *found*.
Frae, *from*.
Gloamin', *twilight*.

Hinnied, *honeyed*.
Kent, *known*.
Maen, *moan*.
Maist, *almost*.
Micht, *might*.
Nae, *no*.
Nane, *none*.

Nicht, *night*.
Nocht, *nought*.
Sic, *at that*.
Siclike, *same*.
Sinsyne, *since then*.
Syne, *then*.
Wae, *mournfully*.

THE LASS O' KINTORE.

AIR—" Oh, as I was kiss'd yestreen!"

At hame or afield I am cheerless an' lone,
I'm dull on the Ury an' droop by the Don;
Their murmur is noisy an' fashious to hear,
An' the lay o' the lintie fa's deid on my ear.
I hide frae the moon, and whaur naebody sees,
I greet to the burnie an' sich to the breeze;
Tho' I sich till I'm silly, an' greet till I dee,
Kintore is the spot in this world for me.
  But the lass o' Kintore, oh, the lass o' Kintore!
  Be warned awa' frae the lass o' Kintore;
  There's a love-luring look that I ne'er kent afore,
  Steals cannily hame to the heart at Kintore.

Afore, *before*.	Fashious, *annoying*.	Lintie, *linnet*.
Awa', *away*.	Frae, *from*.	Naebody, *nobody*.
Dee, *die*.	Greet, *weep*.	Sich, *sigh*.
Deid, *dead*.	Kent, *knew*.	Whaur, *where*.

They bid me forget her—oh! how can it be?
In kindness or scorn she 's ever wi' me;
I feel her fell frown in the lift's frosty blue,
An' I weel ken her smile in the lily's saft hue.
I try to forget her, but canna forget—
I 've liket her lang, an' I aye like her yet;
My poor heart may wither—may waste to its core,
But forget her? oh, never! the lass o' Kintore!
    Oh, the woods o' Kintore! the holmes o' Kintore!
    The love-lichtin' e'e that I ken at Kintore;
    I 'll wander afar, an' I 'll never look more
    On the dark glance o' Peggy or bonnie Kintore!

Canna, *cannot.*
E'e, *eye.*
Ken, *know.*
Lift, *firmament.*
Love-lichtin', *love-kindling.*
Saft, *soft.*
Weel, *well.*

DID THEY MEET AGAIN?

Awa' ye weary licht,
Nae moon nor starnie bricht;
Oh! for thy midwatch nicht
  An' rayless hour;
Whan I may gang alane,
Unmarked by mortal een,
An' meet my bosom queen
  In her murky bower.

I ken she's waitin' there—
She's faithfu' as she's fair—
I'll twine her raven hair
  Roun' her snawie brow;
An' vow by earth an' sea,
Hoo dear she's been to me,
An' thou lone Benachie
  Maun hear that vow.

Alane, *alone*.
Bricht, *bright*.
Een, *eyes*.
Gang, *go*.

Hoo, *how*.
Ken, *know*.
Licht, *light*.

Maun, *must*.
Murky, *dark*.
Nicht, *night*.

We loved—alas! sae leal!
But this sad nicht maun seal
The lang—the last fareweel
   'Tween her an' me.
Whaure'er my fate may guide,
Or weel or wae betide,
I'll mind wha dwalls beside
   Dark Benachie.

Dwalls, *dwells.*   Nicht, *night.*   Wha, *who.*
Leal, *truly.*   Sae, *so.*   Whaure'er, *wherever.*
Maun, *must.*

THE LASS WI' THE WANDERIN' E'E.

"Oh! wha that sang yon sang to me,
    That I can ne'er forget?
Wha is 't that aucht yon lo'esome e'e?
    Sae weel 's I see it yet!
An' cam she frae the far, far east,
    The lass wi' the wanderin' e'e;
The heart lay tremblin' in my breast
    To the sang she sung to me!

"Haud doun sic hope ye fond, fond man,
    For loveless is her strain;
She feasts on hearts aroun' her fa'in,
    Yet scaithless keeps her ain.
She laughs to ken the bleed-drap fa',
    An' gladdens at ilka woun';
Oh, turn your wishfu' heart awa',
    There 's wae in yon sweet soun'!

Ain, *own*.	Fa'in, *falling*.	Sae, *so*.
Aucht, *owns*.	Frae, *from*.	Scaithless, *unhurt*.
Awa', *away*.	Haud, *hold*.	Sic, *such*.
Cam, *came*.	Ilka, *every*.	Wae, *woe*.
Doun, *down*.	Ken, *know*.	Weel, *well*.
Fa', *fall*.		

"I maunna mind what may betide—
    Oh! send that maid to me,
An' place her near this beating side,
    Sae like to gar me dee;
For I would feast on her fair look
    An' lavish on her sang;—
Her dark e'e is a holy book
    In whilk I read nae wrang."

Gar, *make.*
Maunna, *must not.*
Nae, *no.*
Sae, *so.*
Whilk, *which.*
Wrang, *wrong.*

MY HEATHER LAND.

Air—"The Highland Watch."

My heather land, my heather land!
    My dearest pray'r be thine;
Altho' upon thy hapless heath,
    There breathes nae friend o' mine.
The lanely few that Heaven has spar'd
    Fend on a foreign strand;
And I maun wait to weep wi' thee,
    My hameless heather land!

My heather land, my heather land!
    Though fairer lands there be,
Thy gow'nie braes in early days,
    Were gowden ways to me.
Maun life's poor boon gae dark'ning doun,
    Nor die whaur it had dawn'd,
But claught a grave ayont the wave?
    Alas! my heather land!

Ayont, *beyond.*
Braes, *knolls.*
Claught, *catch.*
Doun, *down.*
Fend, *struggle for subsistence.*
Gow'nie, *daisied.*
Maun, *must.*
Whaur, *where.*

My heather land, my heather land!
   Though chilling Winter pours
His freezing breath roun' fireless hearth,
   Whaur breadless misery cow'rs;
Yet breaks the light that soon shall blight
   The godless reivin' hand—
Whan wither'd tyranny shall reel
   Frae our rous'd heather land!

Reivin', *despoiling*.

MY HAMELESS HA'.

Oh! how can I be cheerie in this hameless ha'?
The very sun glints eerie on the gilded wa';
   An' aye the nicht sae drearie,
     Ere the dowie morn daw,
   Whan I canna win to see you
     My Jamie ava.

Tho' monie miles between us, an' far, far frae me,
The bush that wont to screen us frae the cauld warl's e'e,
   Its leaves may waste and wither,
     But its branches winna fa';
   An' hearts may haud thegither,
     Tho' frien's drap awa'.

Ava, *at all*.
Awa', *away*.
Canna, *cannot*.
Cauld, *cold*.
Daw, *dawn*.
Dowie, *gloomy*.

Drap, *fall*.
Eerie, *sadly*.
Fa', *fall*.
Glints, *shines*.
Ha', *hall*.
Haud, *hold*.

Monie, *many*.
Thegither, *together*.
Wa', *wall*.
Warl', *world*.
Win, *get*.
Winna, *will not*.

Ye promis'd to speak o' me to the lanesome moon,
An' weird kind wishes to me, in the lark's saft soun';
    I doat upon that moon,
      Till my very heart fills fu';
    An' aye yon birdie's tune
      Gars me greet for you.

Then how can I be cheerie in the stranger's ha'?
A gowden prison drearie, my luckless fa'!
    'Tween leavin' o' you Jamie,
      An' ills that sorrow me,
    I'm wearie o' the warl'
      An' carena though I dee.

Carena, *care not*.	Gars, *makes*.	Soun', *sound*.
Dee, *die*.	Greet, *weep*.	Warl', *world*.
Fa', *fall, fate*.	Lanesome, *lonesome*.	Weird, *waft*.
Fu', *full*.	Saft, *soft*.	

EXTRACT FROM

A LETTER TO J. ROBERTSON, ESQ.

London, June, 1843.

"INSTANTLY on receipt of yours, expressing a wish to see some of my pieces, I made search and recovered copies of a few which had been printed by friends for private circulation. Enclosed is one piece written about two years ago, my wife lately before having died in childbed. At the time of her decease, although our dwelling was at Inverury, my place of employment was in a village nine miles distant, whence I came once a fortnight, to enjoy the ineffable couthieness that swims around 'ane's ain fireside,' and is nowhere else to be found. For many months, in that we knew comfort and happiness—our daughter Betsy, about ten years of age, was in country service; two boys, younger still, kept at home with their mother. The last Sabbath we ever met, Jean spoke calmly and earnestly of matters connected with our little home and family—bade me remain a day or two with them yet, as she felt a foreboding that the approaching event would be too much for her enfeebled constitution. It was so. She died two days thereafter. On returning from the kirkyard, I shut up our desolate dwelling, and never more owned it as a home. We were but as strangers in the village, so the elder boy and I put over that night in a common tramp house. A neighbour undertook to keep the other little fellow, but he, somehow, slipped away unobserved, and was found fast asleep at the door of our tenantless home. Next morning, having secured a boarding-house for him (the youngest), I took the road to resume labour at the usual place—poor, soft-hearted Willie by my side—a trifle of sad thinking within, and the dowie mists of Benachie right before me. We travelled off our road some miles to the glen where Betsy was 'herdin'.'* Poor Bet knew nothing of what had happened at Inverury. Her mother had visited her three weeks before—had promised to return with some wearables, for winter was setting in fast and bitterly. The day and very hour we approached her bleak residence, *that* was their trysted time. She saw us as we stood on the knowe hesitating—ran towards us—'Oh! whaur is my mither? foo is nae she here? Speak, father! speak, Willie!' Poetry, indeed! Poetry, I fear, has little to do with moments like these. Oh, no! When the bewildering gush has passed away, and a kind of grey light has settled on the ruin, one may then number the drops as they fall, but the cisterns of sorrow echo not when full—hence my idealized address to Willie was written long after the event that gave it existence. With feelings more tranquil, and condition every way better, it came thus:—"

THE ae dark spot in this loveless world,
That spot maun ever be, Willie,
Whaur she sat an' dauted your bonnie brown hair,
An' lithely looket to me, Willie;
An' oh! my heart owned a' the power
Of your mither's gifted e'e, Willie.

There's now nae blink at our slacken'd hearth,
Nor kindred breathing there, Willie;
But cauld and still our hame of Death,
Wi' its darkness evermair, Willie;
For she wha lived in our love, is cauld,
An' her grave the stranger's lair, Willie.

Ae, *one*.
Cauld, *cold*.
Dauted, *patted*.
Evermair, *evermore*.
Hame, *home*.
Lair, *interment*.
Lithely, *warmly*.
Maun, *must*.
Nae, *no*.
Wha, *who*.
Whaur, *where*.

---

* Herdin'—tending cows.

The sleepless nicht, the dowie dawn,
A' stormy though it be, Willie,
Ye 'll buckle ye in your weet wee plaid,
An' wander awa' wi' me, Willie;
Your lanesome sister little kens
Sic tidings we hae to gie, Willie.

The promised day, the trysted hour,
She 'll strain her watchfu' e'e, Willie;
Seeking that mither's look of love,
She never again maun see, Willie;
Kiss ye the tear frae her whitening cheek,
An' speak awhile for me, Willie.

Look kindly, kindly when ye meet,
But speak nae of the dead, Willie;
An' when your heart would gar you greet,
Aye turn awa' your head, Willie;
That waesome look ye look to me
Would gar her young heart bleed, Willie.

Whane'er she names a mither's name,
An' sairly presseth thee, Willie,
Oh! tell her of a happy hame
Far, far o'er earth an' sea, Willie;
An' ane that waits to welcome them,
Her hameless bairns, an' me, Willie.

Ane, *one.*
Bairns, *infants.*
Buckle ye, *wrap yourself.*
Gar, *make.*
Gie, *give.*
Greet, *weep.*
Hae, *have.*
Kens, *knows.*
Nae, *not.*
Nicht, *night.*
Sairly, *sorely.*
Sic, *such.*
Trysted, *appointed.*
Weet, *drenched.*

"I shall just mention another incident, though, in point of order, it should have been told before. After many months of hopeless wanderings, my family and I at length found a settled home at Inverury. Comparative rest and warmth succeeding to watchful misery, we were, one and all, afflicted with dishealth. Willie, especially, suffered long, and at last had to be conveyed to the Aberdeen infirmary. There he had to undergo a serious operation. I knew his timid nature, and went thither to sustain and comfort him through that severe trial. The operation took place a day earlier than that mentioned to me, so it was over ere I arrived. I found him asleep in his little chamber, and the feelings of that moment are partially embodied in the following lines:—"

" Hospital charities for devastated homes! Faugh! Give me my wages; have I not laboured?"

WAKE ye, sleep ye, my hapless boy,
   In this homeless house of care?
Lack ye the warmth of a mother's eye
   On thy *cauldrife*, lonely lair?

Dost thou clasp in thy dream a brother's hand,
   Yet waken thee all alone?
Thy deep dark eye, does it open unblest?
   Nor father?—nor sister? None!

Thy father's board is too narrow my child,
   For ills like thine to be there;
The comfortless hearth of thy parent is cold,
   And his light but the light of despair.

Cauldrife, *cheerless*.   Lair, *bed*.

Has God disown'd them, the children of toil?
　　Is the promise of Heaven no more?
Shall Industry weep?—shall the pamper'd suppress
　　The sweat-earned bread of the poor?

Alas! and the wind as it blew and blew
　　On the famished and houseless then,
Has blighted the bud of my heart's best hope,
　　And it never may blossom again.

Who are they that beat about in the substanceless regions of fancy for material to move a tear? Who but the silken bandaged sons of comfort?—ink-bleeders whose sorrows are stereotyped—they who see life only through the hazy medium of theory, and do at farthest obtain but a mellow blink of those sickening realities that settle around the poor man's hearth.

DREAMINGS OF THE BEREAVED.

The morning breaks bonnie o'er mountain an' stream,
An' troubles the hallowed breath o' my dream!
The gowd light of morning is sweet to the e'e,
But, ghost-gathering midnight, thou'rt dearer to me.
The dull common world then sinks from my sight,
An' fairer creations arise to the night;
When drowsy oppression has sleep-sealed my e'e,
Then bright are the visions awaken'd to me!

Oh! come, spirit mother, discourse of the hours,
My young bosom beat all its beating to yours,
When heart-woven wishes in soft counsel fell,
On ears—how unheedful prov'd sorrow might tell!
That deathless affection—nae trial could break,
When a' else forsook me *ye* wouldna forsake,
Then come, oh! my mother, come often to me,
An' soon an' for ever I'll come unto thee!

An' thou shrouded loveliness! soul-winning Jean,
How cold was thy hand on my bosom yestreen!

Yestreen, *last night*.

'T was kind—for the lowe that your e'e kindled there,
Will burn aye, an' burn, till that breast beat nae mair.
Our bairnies sleep round me, oh! bless ye their sleep,
Your ain dark-e'ed Willie will wauken an' weep;
But blythe in his weepin' he'll tell me how you,
His *heaven-hamed* mammie, was " dautin' his brow."*

Tho' dark be our dwallin'—our happin' tho' bare,
An' night closes round us in cauldness an' care;
Affection will warn us—an' bright are the beams
That halo our hame in yon dear land of dreams.
Then weel may I welcome the night's deathy reign,
Wi' souls of the dearest I mingle me then,
The gowd light of morning is lightless to me,
But, oh, for the night wi' its ghost revelrie!

Bairnies, *children.* Happin', *covering.*
Gowd, *gold.* Heaven-hamed, *whose home is in heaven.*
Lowe, *flame.*

* Patting his forehead.

THE MITHERLESS BAIRN.

When a' ither bairnies are hushed to their hame,
By aunty, or cousin, or frecky grand-dame;
Wha stan's last an' lanely, an' naebody carin'?
'T is the puir doited loonie—the mitherless bairn!

The mitherless bairn gangs till his lane bed,
Nane covers his cauld back, or haps his bare head;
His wee,* hackit heelies are hard as the airn,
An' litheless the lair o' the mitherless bairn!

Aneath his cauld brow, siccan dreams tremble there,
O' hands that wont kindly to kame his dark hair!
But mornin' brings clutches, a' reckless an' stern,
That lo'e nae the locks o' the mitherless bairn!

Airn, *iron.*
Aneath, *beneath.*
Bairnies, *children.*
Cauld, *cold.*
Doited, *confused.*
Frecky, *coaxing.*
Gangs, *goes.*
Hackit, *chapped.*
Haps, *covers.*
Heelies, *heels.*
Ither, *other.*
Kame, *comb.*
Lair, *dwelling.*
Litheless, *comfortless.*
Lo'e nae, *love not.*
Loonie, *boy.*
Nane, *none.*
Puir, *poor.*
Siccan, *such.*
Till, *to.*
Wee, *little.*
Wont, *were accustomed.*

---

* In hardy Scotland, it is not always a sure sign of poverty in its sons and daughters that they are to be seen tripping it bare-footed from April till Christmas. It is choice; but when necessity carries the matter a little farther into the winter, the feet break up in gashes, or "hacks;" hence hackit heelies.

Yon sister, that sang o'er his saftly-rocked bed,
Now rests in the mools whaur her mammie is laid;
The father toils sair their wee bannock to earn,
An' kens nae the wrangs o' his mitherless bairn!

Her spirit, that pass'd in yon hour o' his birth,
Still watches his wearisome wand'rings on earth,
Recording in heaven the blessings they earn,
Wha couthilie deal wi' the mitherless bairn!

Oh! speak him nae harshly—he trembles the while—
He bends to your bidding, and blesses your smile!
In their dark hour o' anguish, the heartless shall learn
That God deals the blow for the mitherless bairn!

Couthilie, *kindly.*
Kens, *knows.*
Mools, *mould.*

Nae, *not.*
Sair, *sore.*
Sang, *sung.*

Wee bannock, *a little bread.*

THE WEDDED WATERS.

Air—"Kind Robin lo'es me."

Gadie wi' its waters fleet,
Ury wi' its murmur sweet,
They hae trysted aye to meet
    Among the woods o' Logie.
Like bride an' bridegroom happy they,
Wooing smiles frae bank an' brae,
Their wedded waters wind an' play
    Round leafy bowers at Logie.

O'er brashy linn, o'er meadow fine,
They never sinder, never tyne,
An' oh! I thought sic meetings mine,
    Yon happy hours at Logie!
But Fortune's cauld an' changefu' e'e,
Gloomed bitterly on mine an' me,
I looket syne, but cou'dna see
    My *sworn* love at Logie.

Now lowly, lanely, I may rue
The guilefu' look, the guilefu' vow,
That fled as flees the feckless dew
    Frae withered leaves at Logie.

Brashy, *rugged*.	Frae, *from*.	Sic, *such*.
Cauld, *cold*.	Hae, *have*.	Sinder, *separate*.
Feckless, *feeble*.	Lanely, *lonely*.	Syne, *then*.
Flees, *flies*.	Linn, *waterfall*.	Tyne, *lose each other*.

But Gadie wi' its torrents keen,*
An' Ury wi' its braes sae green,
They a' can tell how true I 've been
    To my lost love in Logie.

---

  * It is on this stream, which, rising in the parish of Clatt, after a course of some miles, runs into the Ury, the following beautiful song was long ago written, and is well known to all the country :—

" I wish I were whar Gadie rins,
  'Mang fragrant heath and yellow whins,
  Or brawlin' doun the boskie lins,
    At the back o' Bein-na-chie!
Ance mair to hear the wild birds' sang;
To wander birks and braes amang,
Wi' frien's an' fav'rites left so lang
    At the back o' Bein-na-chie.

How mony a day in blythe spring time,
How mony a day in summer's prime,
I've saunterin' whiled awa' the time,
    On the heights o' Bein-na-chie!
Ah! fortune's flowers wi' thorns grow rife,
And walth is won wi' toil and strife;
Ae day gie me o' youthfu' life
    At the back o' Bein-na-chie.

Ah! Mary, there on ilka night,
When baith our hearts were young an' light,
We 've wander'd by the clear moonlight,
    Wi' speech baith fond and free.
Oh! ance, ance mair, whar Gadie rins,
Whar Gadie rins! whar Gadie rins!
Oh! might I die whar Gadie rins,
    At the back o' Bein-na-chie!"

"OH, THAT MY LOVE WAS SO EASILY WON!"*

"Oh, that my love was so easily won!"
   Whaur nae love word was spoken;
Unsought—unwoo'd, my heart had flown—
    I canna hide, I daurna own
   How that poor heart is broken.

"Oh, that my love was so easily won!"
   The gay an' the gallant hae woo'd me;
But he—oh, he never sought to share
    The envied smile, yet mair an' mair
   Yon wordless look subdued me.

Canna, *cannot.*	Mair an' mair, *more and more.*	Nae, *no.*
Daurna, *dare not.*		Whaur, *where.*
Hae, *have.*		

---

* The burden line of a very old song, of which the two following lines are from the wearied lover, who says—

    "I'll buy an auld horse, and I'll hire an auld man,
      And hurl ye back to Northumberlan'."

"Oh, that my Love was so easily won!"
  Oh, that my life would restore him!
He lightlied the love of our pridefu' clan—
  My dreams are fu' o' yon friendless man,
    But the wrath o' my kindred hangs o'er him.

"Oh, that my Love was so easily won!"
  My kin will ye never forgie me?
I've gi'en my heart to a hameless man,
  But I'll wander far frae this friendless lan',
    An' it never mair shall see me.

Forgie, *forgive.*   **Lightlied,** *held cheap.*   **Mair,** *more.*
Gi'en, *given.*

SECOND LOVE.

"The breast that has felt love justly shrinks from the idea of its total extinction as from annihilation itself."

Oh, say not Love will never
   Breathe in that breast again!
That where he bled must ever
   All pleasureless remain.
Shall tempest-riven blossom,
   When fair leaves fall away,
In coldness close its bosom
   'Gainst beams of milder day?
          Oh never, nay!
It blooms where'er it may.

Though ruthless tempest tear—
   Though biting frosts subdue,
And leave no tendril where
   Love's pretty flow'rets grew;
The soil all ravaged so
   Will nurture more and more,
And stately roses blow
   Where daisies droop'd before;
         Then why, oh! why
Should sweet love ever die?

ADDRESS TO THE DON.*

"Will it fair up do you think?" "Aye will 't yet."
                                        GOSSIP.

"The deil and Don came down that day,
　Wi' a' their Highland fury;
An' vowed to 'bear the Bass away,'
　Frae bonnie tremblin' Ury."

DARK Don, thy water's rude repulsive scowl
And frothy margin, all too well bespeak
The upland ravages, the conflict bleak
Of mountain winter; and the maddened howl
Of bruiting elements, distraught and foul,
Have ruffled thy fair course and chok'd thy braes.

---

* Don rises in Strathdon and receives (besides other small rivers) Nochty, from Invernochty; Bucket, from Glenbucket; and Ury from Inverury parishes. It falls into the sea at Old Aberdeen, where it has a fair bridge of one arch, built four ages ago, about A.D. 1320, by king Robert Bruce, while this see was vacant by the flight of Bishop Cheyne—the bridge of Balgownie, celebrated by Lord Byron's

Love flies affrightened at thy swollen look;
The laverock may not hear its own sweet lays
O'er thy fierce chafings, and the timid brook
Sinks tremblingly amid thy surfy maze,
Thou cold remembrancer of wilder human ways!
So soiled the social tide by some curst deed
Of ancient ruffian or fool—so ages read
To weeping worlds of hearts that bled,
Of patriots and sages that have died
Ere that broad stream was half repurified.
Roll thy dark waters, Don—we yet shall see
On thy bright bosom the fair symmetry
Of vaulted heaven, when the shrill lark pours
Voluptuous melody to listening flowers,
And all of man, of earth, and air shall feel
What hate and darkness hurteth, love and light can
    heal!

---

reminiscences. The length of the river Don from above the kirk of Alford is twenty miles, and twenty-four miles from the said kirk to the bridge of Balgownie where Don discharges his streams in the German Ocean close by Old Aberdeen.

The mountain Bennachie, rising with seven tops, on the south is precipitous and rocky, and is a sea mark. The river Ury rising in a low hill, not far from the Castle of Gartly, passing through a sterile valley, whence it struggles through the narrows of the hills, coming down upon the plain which it divides unequally, with its twisting channel, falls into the Don at the little town of Inverury. At the foot and along the whole length of Bennachie, the small stream of the Gadie falls into the Ury a little above the same town.—[Robert Gordon, of Straloch—Description of Sheriffdoms of Aberdeen and Banff, 1654.]

For who so dull that may not now behold
Yon cloud-repelling light, yon moral ray
Piercing the night-born mist, the murky fold,
That erst obscured the intellectual day?
God breathes again in man—those melt, for aye,
Preparing, purifying to the sacred birth
Of virtues hitherto undared on earth.

WHISPER LOW.

Slowly, slowly the cauld moon creeps
   Wi' a licht unlo'esome to see;
It dwalls on the window whaur my love sleeps,
   An' she winna wauken to me.
       Wearie, wearie the hours, and slow,
       Wauken, my lovie, an' whisper low!

There's nae ae sang in heaven's hicht,
   Nor on the green earth doun,
Like soun's that kind love kens at nicht,
   When whispers hap the soun';
       Hearin'—fearin'—sichin' so—
       Whisper, my bonnie lovie, whisper low!

They lack nae licht wha weel can speak
   In love's ain wordless wile;
Her ee-bree creepin' on my cheek
   Betrays her pawkie smile;
       Happy—happy—silent so—
       Breathin'—bonnie lovie, whisper low!

Ee-bree, *eye-brow*.   Pawkie, *sly*.

Was yon a waft o' her wee white han',
  Wi' a warnin' " wheesht" to me?
Or was it a gleam o' that fause moon fa'in'
  On my puir misguided e'e?
    Wearie—wearie—wearie O—
    Wauken, my lovie, an' whisper low!

  Fause, *false.*   Wauken, *waken.*

GLAMOURIE; OR, MESMERISM AS WE HAVE IT AT INVERURY.

Air—"Aiken Drum."

A CARLIE cam' to our toun,
An' bade our drumster rair an' soun',
Till a' the fouk ran rinnin' doun
    T' see fat they could see.

Fat think ye o' the carlie,
The glowrin' fykin' carlie,
The fell auld-fashion'd carlie,
    Wi' a' his glamourie?

Some cam' wi' faith, some cam' wi' fear,
An' monie cam' frae far an' near,
Wi' nae a few that cam' to sneer,
    An' oh, they lookit slee!

Carlie, *little old man.* Fell, *dangerous.* Glowrin', *staring.*
Drumster, *town drummer.* Fouk, *folks.* Rinnin', *running.*
Rair, *roar.* Fykin', *troublesome.* Slee, *sly.*
  Glamourie, *magic.*

An' bureght roun' the carlie,
An' wonnert at the carlie,
An' cried "Fa are ye carlie?
  An' fat a' can ye dee?"

He took my auntie by the thumb,
An' grippet aye my auntie's thumb,
An' aye he squeez'd my auntie's thumb,
  An' glowr'd intill her e'e.

Out fie the fu'some carlie!
The ill contrivin' carlie!
He fumm'lt aye ahint her lug,
  An' ca'ed her "Miss-Meree!"

He faun' ayont the tailor's tap,
An' cam', gweed life! on sic a knap!
His Meggy's heart it flew an' lap,
  For weel I wot kent she.

But aye the rubbin' carlie,
He blew an' blastit sairly,
Till legs an' armies fairly
  Stood stark like ony tree!

Ahint, *behind.*
An' fat a' can ye dee? *and what all can you do?*
Ayont, *behind.*
Bureght roun', *gathered close round.*
E'e, *eye.*
Fa', *who.*
Faun', *felt.*
Fumm'lt, *felt.*
Fu'some, *mischievous.*
Glowr'd, *looked.*
Grippet at, *seized hold of.*
Intill, *into.*
Kent, *knew.*
Lap, *leaped.*
Lug, *ear.*
Miss-Meree, *mesmery.*
Rubbin', *making passes.*
Sic a knap, *such a bump.*
Tap, *head.*
Wonnert, *wondered.*

Ye Debtors deft,—ye Cravers keen,*
Ye Lovers, too, wha roam alane,
Ne'er look ower lang in ither's een,
    In case o' what might be!

For gin ye meet a carlie,
A keekin' cunnin' carlie,
Ye yet may rue richt sairly
    The glamour o' his e'e.

Cravers, *duns*.	E'e, *eye*.	Glamour, *magic*.
Deft, *hard up*.	Gin, *if*.	Keekin', *inquisitive*.

---

* A story was current at Inverury that a creditor (craver) had been mesmerized, and left asleep by his "debtor deft."

SCHOOL OF INDUSTRY.

[A School of Industry exists in the city of Aberdeen, in which destitute orphans, and the children of poverty-stricken parents, are gathered together from the haunts of misery and vice, and put in the way of earning an honest livelihood. Here let curiosity, if not kindness, plead for one visit. If they will not heed yon grim old house, and the helpless outcasts there, then are we not accountable in *whole* for the impiety of wishing that this luckless school had, even at the risk of in-dwelling cormorants, some share in the beef and boilings attached to other nests. But, alas! no droppings here. Here the cook—honest woman!—may lick her fingers as innocently as if she licked a milestone. Nothing in that meagre building to attract an itchy palm—no elegance therein to reward the soft eye of *taste* (?)—nor atone for prunella spoiled; so, happily, neither come. Yet, oh! there is something there will one day speak in words of fire; and when that voice goes forth, happy are they and blessed who have looked in sorrowing kindness on yon shreds of bruised humanity!

"There is hope in heaven—on earth despair."

One thinks it is written on the door, and speaking through each window—so chilly and forlorn looks *our* School of Industry! Yet those cold grey granite walls hold an hundred almost sinless hearts in safety. These, but the other day, were gathered from your lanes and entries—from perdition to peace. There they are—look on them; a fountain amidst a desert of souls—a redemption on earth—the rescued—the snatchings from the kingdom of darkness. Yes; there is a treasure therein will yet speak salvation to the godly minds that placed it there. Ye that care but for the hour that passes, look to your safety—ye heedlessly happy! Know ye not that, in turning the human impulses from a wrong to a right direction, ye are adding to your other sweets the sweet of security; and, by lessening the number of thieves, ye may eat your crowning custard in calmness, and lessen the chances of losing your dear "three courses." Go to yon grim residence of forsaken humanity; look carefully at these sharplike little fellows, and think of your own safety. They came not to *your* world unbidden, and they *will* live. Look at them again—fine, rude, raw material there, ready to be manufactured for better, for worse. Think of the thing in an economical posture. In these hundred boys, as they are being trained, you have an equivalent for a thousand patent locks, forty policemen, four gaols, two transports, and one hangman. Look on these lads again—then turn to that little box, if you have a sigh and a sixpence about you—God bless you, leave the sixpence at any rate! There comes the monitor, leading in two ragged little strangers — brothers they seem. That look of the elder boy searches for one's heart, and should find it too, as his lustrous blue eye fills over his only "kin"—his little brother—already gladdening under the strange comfort of shelter. You gave the sixpence? Well, if the monitor's song please you, give the sigh, too, and "Haste ye back."]

MONITOR'S SONG.

Air—"Prince Charlie's farewell to Skye."

Come Brither bairnies, wan and worn,
And hide ye here frae cauld and scorn;
The blast that tears your weary morn
    May fan your warmer day, boys.

MONITOR'S SONG.

We work and wish, and sich and sing,
And bless the couthie hearts that bring
Ae smile to soothe our surly spring;
   We 'll a' be men when we may, boys!

Your Mither sank before the lave—
Your Father, Sister, sought a grave;
And ye, wee bodies, were left to crave
   A warl's cauldrife care, boys!

But now ye 'll work, and hope, and sing,
Nor needfu' fear how fate may fling;
The Honey may come ahint the Sting,
   And Heaven will send *your* share, boys!

Oh! were the heartless here to see
The wrestling tear that fills your e'e,
Your wee, wee Brith'rie, daft wi' glee,
   Wi' breast and armies bare, boys!

But aft unkent we greet and sing,
And ply the warp and netting string;
Oh! wha would slight that holy thing,
   An orphan's trembling prayer, boys?

Ae, *one.*
Couthie, *kind, loving.*
Greet, *weep.*
Lave, *the rest, the others.*
Sich, *sigh.*
Unkent, *unknown.*
Wee brith'rie, *little brother.*

A hundred hearts are heaving here,
That loup to gladness, grief, and fear;
And *weel* bless they the lips that spier
 How orphans fend and fare, boys!

Oh! blithely work and blithely sing—
There's nane can tell what Time may bring,
Sae freckl'd the feathers that mark his wing,
 So changefu' evermair, boys!

Fend, *make shift.*   Loup, *leap.*   Spier, *ask, inquire.*

THE STRICKEN BRANCH.

[Whoever he is whose destiny leads him from "the spot where he was born," let him prepare for many queer things, even in our own enlightened land. Is he a journeyman weaver? shoemaker? tailor? Then just let him try to set up doing for himself in a small country town. If he does not "*catch it*" then from the brotherhood (brotherhood?), he is one in whom Providence assuredly takes a special interest. In every small community there is a vehement working of the *Keep-out* system, which is only changed for the *Keep-down*. A stranger is never welcome beyond the rule of "*buy and come again.*" The "Income" is a denounced animal. To wrong him in name and property is all for the common weal.

The following is reluctantly inserted to show how far human Ingratitude may be carried—reluctantly, because these verses seem to bear on some vagrant misfortune of the writer, and to reflect on the Sympathy, Justice, and Liberality of our enlightened, Free-trade-loving, Universal-brotherhood-advocating, fellow Burgher, Bailie *Thinclaith*.]

'T was a cauld cauld nicht, and a bauld bauld nicht,
   When the mad wind scoured the plain;
An' monie bonnie bush lay streikit and bare,
   Drown'd deid in the pelting rain.
   The lilac fell a' broken and bent,
   Wi' the leafless woodbine torn and rent;
   And aye as the storm would swither and swell,
   Anither bush brak'—anither bush fell.

Swither, *hesitate, lull.*

A Nettle stood strong in his native mud,
    Rank King o'er his native bog;
He withered aye in the clear daylight,
    But he fattened aye in the fog.
He stung every flow'ret,—cursed every sweet:
He spared nae the Docken that happit his feet;
For this was the song that the auld Nettle sung,
"Darkness and dung, Beetles, darkness and dung!"

[*And the black Beetles chorus it, " Darkness and dung!"*]

In that cauld lang nicht, in that dark lang nicht,
    When the wild winds scoured the plain,
An unkent Branch of an unkent tree
    Was tossed near the Nettle's domain.
An' the weary—weedlike—withering thing,
Lay low at the lair of that Nettle king;
Where nane might dare a byding place,
But that King and his kindred Hemlock race.

The bonniest half o' that Branch sank deid,
    An' its wee, wee bud unseen;
The ither took root an' reared its heid,
    Wi' its twa three Twigs alane.
    Heaven, pitying, held the wild wind fast,
    An' the Stricken Branch out-lived the blast;
The kindly sunbeam settled there,
The branches braid'ning mair and mair;
And monie bonnie bird wi' willing wing,
Had welcome there to nestle and sing.

Docken, *docks.*   Happit, *covered.*   Unkent, *unknown.*

But, oh! how the Nettle grew grim and dark,
   An' fumed in the shadow beneath;
How he bullied his legion of Beetles black!
   An' his Hemlock dews of death!
The Beetles sought sair for a fallen leaf,—
But the hundred eyes of the Hemlock Chief
Could reach no farther than just to see
The deep, deep green of the Stranger Tree.

THE FISHERMEN.

[To record a sympathy in the well-earned gratitude owned by all to Lieutenant Dooley and his brave crew, is the best apology at hand for taking this long hold of the "Herald." I don't know Lieutenant Dooley, nor any other lieutenant, but I know there is more good in saving one fisherman than in sinking seven ships—barring the glory thereof.

"Weel may the boatie row,
And better may she speed."

We had the gratification, on Thursday afternoon, of witnessing one of the most affecting scenes that a person could have much chance of encountering in the course of a long life. It was no less than the meeting of fifty-three fishermen, whose lives had for a time been despaired of by their rejoicing relatives. It was a scene that no philanthropist should have lost, and one that none who witnessed it will be ready to forget.

About four o'clock on the morning of New-year's day, the boats belonging to this port put out to sea, trusting to the appearance of the weather. A part remained inshore, while nine of them made for the deep-water fishing. About six o'clock the moon set in a thick lowering bank in the north-west. The portentous omen was read aright by the fishermen, who, putting "up helm," rowed with might and main for the shore. The boats near the coast succeeded in reaching it; but the others were taken by the hurricane eight miles from land, and, although they struggled on with stout hearts and willing hands, the wind, waves, and blinding snow were all against them, and, instead of making any headway, they drifted before the tempest.

The wives and children, fathers and mothers, of the missing fishermen, looked upon themselves as bereaved of their only earthly support, and the objects of their fondest affection. Of some families there were three, of others four; amissing; and the greater part were more or less connected with one another. To almost every house the touching language of the prophet might have been applied—" There was a voice heard, lamentation, and weeping, and great mourning; Rachel weeping for her children, and refusing to be comforted, because they were not." Through Monday night and Tuesday, this dreadful suspense continued; and eagerly was the post of Wednesday morning waited for, as the *ultimatum* that should extinguish the little remnant of hope that was clung to by the unhappy community, or bring the anxiously prayed for news of the safety of their friends. The preservation of all was scarcely to be looked for, but their fondest hopes were more than realized. Intelligence came that all were safe; and when the glad tidings were carried to Footdee,* the sudden revulsion from the extremity of sorrow to that of joy was evinced by the warmest transports, after a thousand fashions. Some poured forth warm, heartfelt thanks, some weeped, some danced, some sang; but one feeling animated all—the deepest, purest, and most intense joy that can fall upon the heart of man.

The fishermen, after struggling for hours against the tempest, lost all hope of outliving it. Their boats were fast filling with water, and becoming entirely unmanageable; and, even had there been any possibility of working them, the poor men, with a few exceptions, were unable to stir themselves; they had become completely exhausted, and so benumbed with the piercing cold, as to be incapable of handling their oars. Death, in two forms, was staring them in the face, certain in the one or other. There was help at hand, however, when least expected. The *Grey-*

---

* The fishing station.

hound cutter on this station, commanded by Lieutenant Dooley, while running before the wind, came in sight of the boats about eleven o'clock, off Findonness, and bore up to them. The greatest difficulty existed in taking the men from their frail crafts. Some of them were old and feeble, and in such a state, from wet and exposure, that made it necessary, as seamen say, to "parbuncle" them; while the storm had risen to such a height that the mainsail of the cutter was carried away, and her work of mercy in some measure retarded. A trysail was, however, soon hoisted in its place, and, after an hour or two, the whole of the poor men were stowed away in warm berths or dry clothing, and all their wants most kindly attended to by the warm-hearted commander and his gallant crew. Nor did their endeavours cease with the preservation of the lives of the fishermen; every attempt was made to save their property likewise. The boats were all made fast astern by a five-inch hawser, but the increasing storm dashed them one by one against another, stove them in, and soon rendered it necessary to set them adrift. The cutter then made for the Frith of Forth, and the whole of the fishermen were landed at Leith.

At four o'clock on Thursday afternoon, the whole of the fishermen reached their homes, when the scene was the most touching that could be imagined. About six or seven hundred in all were present—young and old—men, women, and children.—*Aberdeen Herald.*]

LINES SUGGESTED BY THE ABOVE DISASTER.

'T was the blythe New Year, when hearts are mov'd,
   Like fairy wind harp ringing,
To the breathing smile of friend belov'd,
In whisper dear—in noisy cheer—
Nae fash, nae fear—the good New Year
   Sets the good old world asinging.

But, oh! it is dark in the fisherman's cot,
   With the lively and lovely there;
Tho' the cold, cold wind, with its icy throat,
Falls fiercely—yet one hears it not,
   Thro' sob, and sigh, and prayer.

So that should be—when the terrible sea
   Speaks woe to the trembling earth—
Hope wing'd away with the closing day,
Now cold despair wraps all things there,
   And scowls o'er the fisherman's hearth.

Man dies but once—oh, say it not!
   He lives again to die,
Whom the surly, surly sea has taught
   The hope-dissolving sigh;
When the stubborn arm that strains for life
   Falls feebly on the oar;
When the loved last look of child and wife
Swims wildly o'er the settling strife,
   Oh, Death! what canst thou more?

LINES TO MISS LUCY LAWRENCE OTTLEY.

Written at Naish, July, 1841.

You may not love the lay
   Unhallow'd by a tear,
And she that's far away
   Claims all that I can spare;
But when I let her ken,
   How you have pleasured me,
She winna grudge it then
   Ae parting tear to thee.

When other hours recall
   The joys that I ha'e seen
In England's happy hall,
   On England's flowery green,
When my own native lark
   Floats o'er my native lea,
What can I then but mark
   Its kindred melody?

LINES TO MISS OTTLEY.

For never yet mair sweet,
   Has lark or mavis sung;
And, oh! that face to meet
   That saftly witching tongue!
My lastening heart will prize
   Your sang o' sweetness mair
Than carrols frae the skies,
   Wi' a' its gladness there.

My lowland lassie sings
   Far sweeter than the rest;
And a' her leal heart rings
   In sangs that I love best.
Sae whan her soul-filled strain
   Fa's trembling on my ear,
Oh! but I'll mind them then,—
   The sangs you sung me here.

When o'er thy violet brow,
   And on thy changing cheek,
And 'neath that breast of snow,
   A thousand throbbings speak.
Oh, may the favoured ane
   Thy fair perfections see!
And love with love alane
   Befitting heaven and thee.

KNOCKESPOCK'S LADY.

[An ancestor of JAMES ADAM GORDON, Esq., the present Laird of Knockespock, (*a*) about a century and a half ago, in a second marriage, had taken to wife the lovely Jean Leith of Harthill (*b*). His affectionate lady watched the chamber of her sick husband by day and by night, and would not divide her care with any one. Worn out and wasted from continued attendance on him, she fell into a sleep, and was awakened only by the smoke and flames of their burning mansion; the menials had fled—the doom of the dying laird and his lady seemed fixed. In her heroic affection she bore her husband from the burning house, laid him in a sheltered spot, and forced her way back to the tottering stair, through the very flames, for "plaids to wrap him in."]

AE wastefu' howl o'er earth an' sea,
   Nae gleam o' heaven's licht
Might mark the bounds o' Benachie (*c*)
   That black and starless nicht.
Siclike the nicht, siclike the hour,
   Siclike the wae they ken,
Wha watch till those lov'd eyes shall close
   That ne'er may ope again.

Licht, *light*.   Siclike, *suchlike*.   Wae they ken, *sorrow*
Nicht, *night*.   Wha, *who*.   *they feel.*

KNOCKESPOCK'S LADY.

As gin to tak' the last lang look,
   He raised a lichtless e'e;
Now list, oh, thou, his lady wife,
   Knockespock speaks to thee!
"Sit doun, my Jeanie Gordoun love,
   Sit doun an' haud my head;
There 's sic a lowe beneath my brow
   Maun soon, soon be my dead.

"Aye whaur ye find the stoun, oh, Jean!
   Press there your kindly hand;
I wadna gi'e ae breath o' thee
   For a' else on my land.
Your couthie word dreeps medicine,
   Your very touch can heal;
An', oh, your e'e does mair for me
   Than a' our doctor's skill!"

She leant athwart his burnin' brow,
   Her tears lap lichtly doun;
Beneath her saft, saft, dautin' hand
   Knockespock sleepit soun'.
For woman's watch is holiness—
   In woman's heart, sae rare,
When a' the warld is cauld an' dark,
   There 's licht an' litheness there!

A', *all.*
Ae, *one.*
Couthie, *kindly.*
Dautin', *fondling.*
Gin, *if.*
Haud, *hold.*
Lichtless, *desponding.*
Lap lichtly, *leaped lightly.*
Licht, *light.*
Litheness, *warmth.*
Lowe, *burning.*
Mair, *more.*
Maun, *must.*
Sic, *such.*
Stoun, *throbbing pain.*
Wadna gie, *would not give.*
Whaur, *where.*

What 's yon that tints the deep dark brae,
   An' flickers on the green?
It 's nae the ray o' morning grey,
   Nor yet the bonnie meen!
Drumminor's(*d*) bloody Ha' is bright,
   Kildrummie's(*e*) sna' tower clear,
An' Noth's(*f*) black Tap ca's back the licht
   To gowden Dunnideer.(*g*)

Yon gleed o'er fast and fiercely glows,
   For licht o' livin' star,
An' lo! it marks wi' giant brows,
   The murky woods o' Mar.(*h*)
The drowsy deer is fain to flee,
   Beyond Black Arthur's(*i*) hicht;
An' birdies lift a timorous e'e,
   To yon ill-bodin' licht.

Whaur Bogie(*k*) flows, and Huntly(*l*) shows
   On high its lettered wa's;
An' westward far on Cabrach's(*m*) breast,
   The ruddy glimmerin' fa's.
Whaur monie a Forbes and Gordoun sleeps,
   On Tillyangus(*n*) deein';
An' Mar's road sweeps, 'mid their cairn's grey
   heaps,
   The fiery flakes are fleein'.

Ca', *casts*.   Licht, *light*.   Meen, *moon*.
Gleed, *glare*.

An' aye the flare that reddens there,
    Knockespock weel may rue;
Nor Gadie's(o) stream can dit the gleam
    That wraps his dwallin' noo.
Yet woman's love, Oh, woman's love!
    The wide unmeasured sea
Is nae so deep as woman's love,
    As her sweet sympathy!

Upon the wet an' windy sward
    She wadna lat him down,
But wiled an' wiled the lithest beild
    Wi' breckans happet roun'.
Knockespock's cauld, he's deadly cauld—
    Whaur has his lady gane?
How has she left him trembling there,
    A' trembling there alane?

An' has she gane for feckless gowd,
    To tempt yon fearfu' lowe?
Or is her fair mind, wreck'd an' wrang,
    Forgane its guidance now?
She fearless speels the reekin' tow'r,
    Tho' red, red is the wa',
An' braves the deaf'nin' din an' stour,
    Whaur cracklin' rafters fa'.

Alane, *alone*.
Beild, *spot*.
Breckans, *bushes*.
Cauld, *cold*.
Din, *noise*.
Dit, *stop*.
Dwallin', *dwelling*.
Fa', *fall*.
Feckless, *feeble*.

Forgane, *forgone*.
Gowd, *gold*.
Happet, *covered*.
Lithest, *warmest*.
Lowe, *blaze*.
Nae, *not*.
Reekin', *smoking*.
Roun', *over*.

Speels, *climbs*.
Stour, *dust*.
Wa', *wall*.
Wadna, *would not*.
Whaur, *where*.
Weel, *well*.
Wiled, *chose*.
Wrang, *wrong*.

It is na gowd, nor gallant robes,
   Gars Jeanie Gordoun rin;
But she has wiled the saftest plaids
   To wrap her leal lord in.
For woman's heart is tenderness,
   Yet woman weel may dare
The deftest deed, an' tremble nane,
   Gin true love be her care.

"The lowe has scaith'd your locks, my Jean,
   An' scorch'd your bonnie brow;
The graceless flame consumes our hame—
   What thinks my lady now?"
"My locks will grow again, my love,
   My broken brow will men',
Your kindly breast's the lealest hame
   That I can ever ken;

"But, Oh, that waesome look o' thine,
   Knockespock, I wad gi'e
The livin' heart frae out my breast
   For aught to pleasure thee!"
Weel, woman's heart! ay, woman's heart!
   There grows a something there,
The sweetest flower on bank or bower
   Maun nane wi' that compare.

Aught, *anything*.
Deftest, *boldest*.
Frae, *from*.
Gars, *makes*.
Gi'e, *give*.
Gin, *if*.
Ken, *know*.
Leal, *true*.
Maun, *must*.
Nane, *not*.
Rin, *run*.
Waesome, *woeful*.
Weel, *well*.
Wiled, *chose*; Aberdonicè, for *waled*.

NOTES.

[Lest the reader mistake me as aspiring at Scholarship in the following notes, let me say this,—they were selected * and proposed by my friend Knockespock. In assenting to his insertion of them, I decline all responsibility.—W. T.]

Knockespock—Burns—Highland Harry.

(a) Knockespock. ("Bishop's Hill"), so called from having been the occasional residence of the Roman Catholic bishops of Aberdeen, is situated to the north of the Suie Hill, a continuation of the western shoulder of Benachie in the parish of Clatt, of which last the Barony was conferred by James I. of England and VI. of Scotland "on his well-beloved James Gordoun of Knockespoke." Clatt was erected into a Burgh of Barony with all rights, &c. by King James IV. in 1501, some years previous to the Battle of Flodden. The ancient mansion having been destroyed by fire, as the Poet herein describes, nothing remains of it but one old tower, the rest of the mansion being of modern construction. The water is remarkable for its purity, and on accurate analysis proves to be more pure than that of Malvern.

In the poem of Surgundo, written on the exploits of Sir Adam Gordon, of Auchindoun, in which the letters of every name are quaintly transposed, there are the following verses on one of the possessors of Knockespock:—

"Four of most famous note the rest among
For valiant acts in many a bloody fight,
Paesenneock truely termed the loyall knight."—p. 29.

"Loyall Pasennock ———
——— aids him mightilie."—p. 61.

The domestic affairs of Knockespock have many years ago been the subject of verse, in a lilt which records the unfortunate results which attended an attachment between Henry Lumsden, and a daughter of a lady of Knockespock, ending in the death of the

---

* Chiefly from the Spalding Club Volumes; The Advocates' Library MS.; popular traditions; Buchanan; County Records; Songs, Lilts, &c.—K.

Burns' Uncle Burnes—Harthill—Leith of Harthill.

lover, and the despair of the lady. In the country, far and near, it is still recited. The burden of her remonstrances to her mother, of

" I wad gie a' Knockespock's land,
    For ane shake of Harry's hand,"

is natural and pathetic, and so pleased the poet Burns, that he transferred it as a chorus to his song of "Highland Harry." Most of Burns' editors have applied it to a farm of almost the same name, Knockespie, near one of Burns' residences in Ayrshire, but Allan Cunningham in his edition has placed the whole matter correctly, and shown that those lines existed before Burns was born, and the source whence he derived them.

Burns, on his first visit to Aberdeenshire called on an uncle Burnes, whom he had never before seen, and whose descendants, Burnesses, yet reside on the same farm, at Boghead, near Inverury,—showed his MSS. to the cannie auld farmer, and mentioned his intention of publishing. The uncle was silent a while, unable to utter the horror working within. At last it burst forth,—"Worthless, senseless man! how could ye think o' bringing a stain on kith and kin', by makin' Godless ballets?" Happily for the world, unhappily perhaps for himself, his advice displeased the poet. A late servant of the writer of this, Matthew Sharpe Glendinning, informs him that when a boy in Dumfries he perfectly remembers Burns as an exciseman coming to his mother's house.

At Knockespock is a very large sword several feet in length, almost a fac simile of the one carried before Prince Charles Edward in 1745, exhibited in the Tower of London, but destroyed in the fire there a few years since, and some carved panels of arms of 1632. The highway from Edinburgh to Inverness passes by Knockespock, little used of late years except by cattle drovers. The Highland distillery line passes close by the mansion.

(*b*) Harthill, a castle long possessed by the Leiths of Harthill, chiefs of that name, the heir of which family was beheaded at the Cross of Edinburgh, for his loyalty, by the Marquis of Argyle, 26th October, 1647, being scarce 25 years old, having been taken prisoner with his garrison in the house of Wardes close to Dunnideer, by the celebrated General David Lesley. It is reported of him, that having obtained a commission from the Marquis of Montrose, but having no horses to mount his troop, and hearing that Craigivar of the opposite party with his troop were lying at Inverury, by night made all prisoners, and with their horses mounted his own troop, making a good appearance in a day or two before Montrose, who highly com-

Benachie—Camp—Roman Road—Moneymusk —Aldivalloch—Logie o' Buchan—Lochnagar—Drumminor—Forbes—Ariosto.

---

mended his conduct and courage. There is also a more affecting history connected with this old castle, namely, that while Harthill was imprisoned at Edinburgh, his castle was beset, and his wife, children, and servants taken out, and shot one by one before the gate. The walls bear evident marks of fire, being rent in several places from top to bottom, yet they are erect, very strong, being about five feet thick, and forty feet high, with round towers, bartisans, loopholes, an arched gateway and turret, and chimney vents above ten feet wide. This ancient ruin stands forward under the dark screen of Benachie, so as to attract the attention of the traveller along the high road from Inverury westward, from which it lies a mile distant.

(c) "*Might mark the bounds of Benachie.*"

Benachie, the chief hill in the Garioch is Benachie, a mountain about seven miles long, it has seven heads, the chief of which being a round peak, is called the top.

On the highest point is an immense British Camp which had been used by the Romans when wrested from the natives. A causeway road may still be traced up the north side of the hill to it, which, beyond all doubt, is a Roman work. (See the note to the Blind Boy's Second Prank, page 58.) Benachie signifies the hill of the paps or nipples from Ben, or Pen, a head, and Chiod, a nipple (Gaelic). It is a sea mark. An old verse says,—

"There are two landmarks off at sea,
Clochnabin and Benachie."

It was one of the king's forests of old.

On the south it is precipitous, and overhangs the river Don and the fertile vale of Moneymusk—Moneymusk known favourably to the dancing world by its spirited Strathspey. In fact Benachie is surrounded by spots redolent of harmony,—Aldivalloch, Logie o' Buchan, The Gadie Rins, and Mill o' Tiftie's Annie. Of late it has been ascertained that there were singing schools in every parish three or four hundred years ago, and the church music of the cathedral of Aberdeen was so celebrated that foreigners resorted thither to hear it; the very motto of the town, "Bon Accord," smacks of music.

From the top of Benachie, and in the same county of Aberdeen, the dark "Lochnagar," which inspired George Gordon, Lord Byron's muse, is clearly seen in the remoter Highlands.

(d) "*Drumminor's bloody ha'.*"

Druminnor, for many centuries the chief residence of the Forbes family, and called Castle Forbes till it was sold off, when it resumed

NOTES.

Feast at Drumminor—Robert Bruce.

its ancient Gaelic name, and the name of Castle Forbes was given to the present seat of Putachie, in the parish of Keig, close to the river Don. The name was pronounced For-bes, which is consistent with the verse of Ariosto—

" Signoria Forbesse il forte Armano."
Orlando Furioso.

who describes the clan as joining Charlemagne's army against the Saracens.

A reconciliation feast was once held there, to which their hereditary enemies the Gordons being invited were seated alternately with the Forbeses. The "toddy" having got uppermost in the noble Forbes's upper story, in a fit of oblivious delight he stroked his venerable beard—a signal hitherto understood to convey a hint, that each Forbes should make the ribs of his neighbour acquainted with his dirk. The hint was taken, and the Gordons rolled in their gore.

Great portion of the ancient castle was destroyed by fire, but the entrance tower still remains of red sandstone, with three coats of arms over the thick iron-studded door to a winding stair of easy and wide ascent. The walls are enormously thick; a handsome and convenient mansion has been attached by the present possessor, Mr. Foularton Grant, in the Elizabethan or James I. style.

In the adjoining kirkyard of Kearn, it is said that sixteen barons of Forbes are buried. The estate marches with that of Knockespock. Druminnor lies within a mile of Rhynie, celebrated for its cattle fair, and where Macbeth's sons were slain, and about three miles from the summit of the Tap of Noth, which is seen to the greatest advantage from it.

(e) " Kildrummie's sna' tower clear."

This castle, a royal palace, the chief seat of the Earls of Mar, in which district of Aberdeenshire it stands, is in ruins, but some remains of it are very interesting. The " sna tower " is built of a white stone, whence its name. This castle, so remote among the hills, was the refuge of Robert Bruce's queen and his brother Nigel; but being besieged by the Earl of Salisbury, it was taken, and they were made prisoners. Nigel was hung at Berwick, by hated Edward, as a traitor! and the queen inhumanly treated. Near the castle is a pleasant shooting-lodge of Colonel C. Gordon, of Wardhouse. It was the centre of Mar's rebellion in 1715. The

Kildrummie—Tap of Noth—Dunnideer—Arthur's Round Table.

church is distant; and in 1813 had a tomb of one of the Erskines, Earl of Mar, and his Countess.

Near Kildrummie are a large number of Pictish houses under ground, of most curious construction, which are often visited.

Kildrummie is about seven miles from Knockespock, by the Mar Road.

(f) "Noth's black Tap."

The Tap of Noth is a lofty eminence, rising to a green cone at the western end of its dark heather ridge. It is surmounted by an area, surrounded with the debris of vitrified fortifications, which are coalblack. There are only two others like it in Scotland, one Craig Phatric, near Inverness; some have thought it an extinct volcano, and its form is favourable to the conjecture; and there are found small masses of vitrified matter at some miles around; but the fort seems undeniable. The Bogie runs at its foot, and it forms one of the entrance hills to Strathbogie.

In the midst of the vitrified fort of the Tap, which may cover about one and a half acre, there is a well.

This mountain, with the greater part of the surrounding country to the north and west, is the property of the Duke of Richmond, the heir of the Dukes of Gordon.

(g) "To gowden Dunnideer."

Dunnideer. On a lofty green conical hill stand the ruins of the castle of Dunnideer, looking at a distance like a huge Druidical remain. It was built by King Gregory, who died here 893. There is a tradition that the hill has gold ore under it, because the sheep's teeth which feed upon it turn yellow, and that the name of the hill, Doun d'or, signifies the golden mount. The castle is built in the midst of a vitrified fort.

In Jhon Hardyng's map of Scotland, constructed about the year 1465, appear "the castells of Strabolgy, of Rithymay, of Dony Dowre;" and the writer seems to indicate the place as one of those where King Arthur held his Round Table, so famous in old romance:—

> "He held his household and the Rounde Table
> Sometyme at Edinburgh, sometyme at Striveline,
> Of Kynges renowned and most honourable;
> At Carlysle sumwhile, at Alcluid his citie fyne,
> Emong all his Knightes and Ladies full femenine;
> And in Scotlande, at Perthe and Dunbrytain,
> In Cornwaile also, Dover, and Cairelegion;

Mar—Earls of Mar—Mar's Rebellion, 1715.—Ariosto—Buchan.

> At Dunbar, Dunfirse, and St. John's Toune,
> All of worthy Knights moo than a legion,
> At Donydoure also in Murith region,
> And in many other places both Citie and Toune."

(h) "*The murky woods of Mar.*"

Mar, the Highland district of Aberdeenshire, very extensive and mountainous. In the forest of Mar, in the very heart of the Highlands, are the celebrated Scotch firs in the midst of the most splendid scenery imaginable. It was under the pretence of great hunting matches in this remote district, that Erskine, Earl of Mar, whose chief seat was the castle of Kildrummie, concocted the Rebellion of 1715, which ended in his ruin and confiscation. The Earldom had been in the family of the Mars, which, having reckoned nine earls, ended under King David the Second. Through a daughter it came to the Earls of Douglas, then the Stewarts, then the Erskines, the Cochranes, and to James Stuart the Regent, Earl of Murray, natural brother to Queen Mary, who restored it to the Erskines. James the Eighth created the last John Earl of Mar a Duke in 1715, thus fulfilling Ariosto's prophecy two hundred years previously, who in his Orlando Furioso writes, on the muster of the Scottish auxiliaries sent over to Charlemaine,

> " L'altra bandiera è del Duca di Marra."

and again,

> " Trasone intanto, il buon Duca di Marra,
> Che ritrovarsi all' alta impresa gode.
> Ai cavalieri suoi leva la sbarra,
> E seco invita alle famose lode."
>
> *Orlando Furioso.*

Mar is a regality; it abounds with red deer. The writer saw in the church of Kildrummie, in 1813, a flat stone, with the effigies of one of the Erskines, Earl of Mar, and his Countess. The forfeited estates were computed at 1678*l.* sterling, of which only 317*l.* were paid in money, the rest being paid in barley, oatmeal, capons, hens, chickens, geese, linen, and peats.

Aberdeenshire has been peculiarly honoured by Ariosto; not only has Mar been recorded in his Orlando, and as we have just seen the clan of the Forbes's, but the following lines refer to Buchan and its Earl :—

> " Quell' avoltór che un drago verde lania,
> El' insegna del conte di Boccania."
>
> *Orlando Furioso.*

Black Arthur, of Forbes', Cairn — Bogie river — Strathbogie — Alexander, Duke of Gordon — Huntly.

(*i*) "*Beyond Black Arthur's hicht.*"

Black Arthur's hicht. One of the highest hills in this part of the country, covered with heather to the top, is called Arthur's Cairn, some suppose from a cairn or sepulchral heap being raised to the memory of Black Arthur of Forbes, who, it is reported, by way of exercise used to run up to the top of it from Druminnor (then Castle Forbes) in heavy armour. He was slain in the battle of Tillyangus, hereafter mentioned.

(*k*) "*Where Bogie flows.*"

Bogie. The river Bogie rises in a wild hill glen, called Glenbogie, and passing by Rhynie—on the moor of which it is said the sons of Macbeth were slain (as also that Macbeth himself died at Lumphanan, a parish a few miles distant)—flows some dozen miles down the Strath, which takes its name from it, recently rather celebrated for its Fast and Free Kirk differences, until it falls into the Deveron under the walls of Huntly Castle, which however, as well as the town around it, used to be called Strathbogie. It was from this vale that the best warriors of the Gordon clan were taken, and there is a very old defiance of—

" Wha wou'd misca' a Gordoun on the raes o' Strathbogie?"

There is nothing picturesque in this fertile valley, unless it be the windings of the Bogie, so remarkable for its peculiarly blue colour; whereas the Deveron into which it falls is very dark.

It would not be just, or grateful, in the writer to omit mention here of the well known Song, composed by Alexander, late Duke of Gordon, one of the best musicians and lively poets in that line of ballads :—

" There's cauld kail in Aberdeen,
 There's castocks in Strathbogie,
And monie a lad maun hae his lass,
 But I maun hae my cogie." * &c. &c.

In Duke Alexander, the Poet might, and *would*, have found a patriotic patron, who from his own could duly estimate the worth and genius of others.

" Hunc saltem accumulem donis et fungar inani,
" Munere !"

(*l*) " ——— *and Huntly shows
On high its lettered walls.*"

Huntly. This castle is one of the finest ruins in Scotland. It in fact consists of two castles—one, the oldest, Strathbogie Castle,

---

* Cogie, *a drinking cup.*

Cummin—Lochaber—Badenoch—Castle of Tours.

the stronghold of the Cummin, whom Robert Bruce stabbed at the altar of Dumfries, and who, on the Bruce proving victorious, forfeited his immense possessions, which were made over by that king to his faithful follower Gordon, in whose descendants it has continued ever since, though by marriages with females the present family are Setons, and the real head of the clan by the males is Gordon of Pitlurg. To show the extent of the possession, which may be said to stretch across the island from the east coast of Aberdeenshire to Ben Nevis on the west, in 1813, the writer was informed that the Duke could ride in almost a straight line for one hundred and forty miles on his own property. Since that the Gordons have bid "farewell to Lochaber" and to "Badenoch," after having been lords of them for five hundred years, they having been sold off. On the occasion of the late Duke's marriage the writer sat down at Gordon Castle with forty-four gentlemen of the name, all of considerable landed property; and to show how widely it is diffused in Aberdeenshire, his was the forty-ninth of that name on the roll of magistrates of that county.

The other castle joining to the former was built in 1602, and was habitable till within the last fifty years, when one of the duke's factors in his absence despoiled it of its roof and a great part of its freestone masonry to repair farm-houses! The round tower, very lofty, and ornamented, with walls of tremendous thickness, capable of sustaining heavy cannon, reminds the traveller of some of the towers of Heidelburgh; and it is said that it was built by an Earl of Huntly, who, having been banished by party feud, was made governor of the castle at Tours, in France, and built this on a similar plan. The sculpture, over the low but principal entrance, of coats of arms and figures, though much defaced, is still remarkable for its execution; but the chimney-piece in the grand saloon, nearly twenty feet high, displaying the arms and orders of the two *then* United Crowns, with the different family arms, and mottoes, and legends, with two figures in armour, one leaning on the great Highland double-handed sword, the other with the Scottish pike flanking both sides of the fire-place, and supporting the entablature, all executed in the red and white stone of the country, may well vie for design, for colouring, and for feudal associations, with any chimney-piece at Hatfield, or Burleigh, or any houses in England of a similar date and style of architecture. The display of the Royal arms, carved in stone over the great hall chimney-pieces in this castle, in Craigievar, and the oldest castles in Scotland, confirms the address of the old Earl of Angus to Lord Marmion, at Tantallon.—

Huntly Castle—Lettered walls—Doings of Earls of Huntly—Buck of the Cabrach—Ordnance Survey—Craig.

> " My castles are my king's alone,
> From turret to foundation-stone."

Along the curtain of this magnificent building, and about sixty feet from the ground, run two parallel bands of stone, on which are inscribed in Roman capital letters of two feet in height,

" GEORGE GORDOUN, FIRST MARQUESS OF HUNTLY,"
" HENRIETTA STEUART, FIRST MARQUISE OF HUNTLY."

Hence the " lettered walls." In the interior of the castle there are several carved chimney-pieces in stone, one of which, supposed to be in the state bed-room, represents the effigies, nearly the size of life, of the founder and his haughty wife. Some of the feudal and almost unmentionable proceedings of some of the ladies of this castle, and of its lords too, as relating to the clans Grant and Macintosh, not to mention others, may be found in Sir Walter Scott's Tales of a Grandfather, and tend to reconcile one to living in an age of Railways and Steam when the humblest weaver may indulge his poetical fancy, and delight with his effusions the trans-Atlantic and far distant Indian worlds, without having his head or hands chopped off for the offence.

(m) " *An' far far west on Cabrach's breast.*"

Cabrach. There is another version of this stanza too true to nature and poetry to be omitted.

> It whitens o'er the gladless grey,
> Of Cabrach's rugged breast,
> But Tillyangus' bloody brae
> Frowns redder than the rest."

The Buck of the Cabrach is the highest mountain in these parts, rising gradually to a point. At the foot of it lies the burn, and what was once the mill of Aldivalloch, but of Roy's wife's habitation there remains nothing but the hearth stone.

On the summit of the Cabrach is one of the stations for the triangular ordnance survey, which, although it has been thirty years about, does not seem to have done much, although the country are paying largely for it. The country about here is very backward, and it is said that if they can save one crop out of four, they consider themselves well off! The burn of the Cabrach descends to the eastward through the picturesque glen, and immediately under the House of Craig, allowed to be the most romantic

Arthur Johnston, poet of Caskieben—Lines ad Gordonium Cragachindorium—Auchindore Chapel.

and beautifully kept place in that part of the country, and a little lower down under the ruins and burying-ground of the ancient church of Auchindoir, (of which, however, the beauties can hardly be discovered, owing to its being enveloped in ivy, and looking more like a bush than a ruin,) falls into the Bogie. Arthur Johnston thus addresses Gordon of Craig, otherwise Gordonium Cragachindorium:—

> " Siccine, Gordoni, Cabriis affixus ericis,
>   Urbe procul, rupes inter, et antra, lates?
> Quid juvat ingenio genium vicisse Minervæ,
>   Ingenii dotes si sinis usque premi?
> Quid juvat, Aoniæ fontes siccasse cohortis,
>   Si fruitur studiis Cabria sola tuis?
> Quid prodest, mores hominum vidisse, vel urbes,
>   Nulla tuam si res publica sentit opem?
> Hic ubi tu latitas, nil præter lustra ferarum,
>   Et cœli volucres, saxaque surda vides.
> Nullum hic, qui doctas haurire aut reddere voces,
>   Aut a te quidquam discere possit, habes.*
> Barbara gens tota est, et inhospita terra, pruinis
>   Semper, et æstivo sub Cane, mersa nive."
>   &c. &c.

The poet was born at Caskieben, a castle belonging to his family, situated on a rising ground, a few hundred yards east of Keithall, close upon Inverury. Describing his native place, he writes:—

> " Mille per ambages nitidis argenteus undis
>   Hic trepidat lœtos Urius inter agros.
> Explicat hic seras ingens Bennachius umbras
>   Nox ubi libratur lance diesque pari.
> Gemmifer est amnis, radiat mons ipse lapillis," &c.

Arthur Johnston received the degree of M.D. at Padua, 1610, and settled in France. In 1633 he returned to his native country, was appointed physician to Charles I., and died at Oxford, 1641. The classical elegance of his verse, and the purity of his Latin in his translation of the Psalms, and his other poems, has been long acknowledged. Arturi Johnstoni, Poemata omnia, p. 362. A new edition is about to appear.

---

* Not only voices, words, but even sentences, are reported to have been heard occasionally in the ruined chapel of Auchindoir, which have created great interest, and some alarm. Does the poet allude to them?

Cabrach—Six Scotch Knights—Tillyangus—Surgundo—Last clan battle in Scotland—Forbes and Gordon—Black Arthur slain.

The Cabrach must have been the very cradle of those six valiant knights, who for so many centuries effectually fought for, and maintained the Honour and Independence of Scotland.

> "Three Knights fair Scotland did defend,—
> Sir Moss, Sir Muir, Sir Mountain;
> Three more to these their aid did lend,—
> Sirs Hunger, Cold, and Dountin'."*

(n) "*On Tillyangus deein'.*"

Tillyangus. This place, formerly a lairdship, is about a mile and a half from Knockespock, and now belongs to that property.

Here was fought, October 9, 1571, the last regular clan battle in Scotland between the Gordons and the Forbes's, on the heather above the present toun (as it is called in Scotland), which means generally a small cluster of habitations.

John, Master of Forbes, who stood up for James VI., then a minor, had one hundred and twenty of his men surprised and killed by Sir Adam Gordon, of Auchindoun, Huntly's brother, who fought for Mary (Queen of Scots). The political differences of these great clans had been aggravated by the ill conduct of Forbes to his wife, who was sister to the Earl of Huntly. Tillyangus lies a mile and a half from Knockespock, where the Gordons coming from the south to go northwards to their own country, mustered for several weeks, while the Forbeses had their outpost half way between Tillyangus and Castle Forbes (Drumminor). At length they met— The Gordons were far more numerous than the Forbeses. This, however, was compensated by the bravery of Black Arthur, second brother to the Lord Forbes, a man of a daring and active temper, who was completely armed, and slew many of the Gordons with his own hand. After a gallant fight the Forbeses gave way, retiring towards Castle Forbes. Black Arthur, with a chosen few, protected their rear. In crossing one of the small rills descending from the hills he was slightly wounded, and it is said was offered quarter, which he refused, fighting on, till in his retreat he crossed the hollow of another small burn. Here, overcome with thirst, he stooped to drink, and by doing so an opening in the joints of the armour was made, through which one of his pursuers coming rapidly upon him thrust his sword and killed him. The Gordons now followed rapidly their flying foes, who took refuge in Castle Forbes. After two days

---

* Dountin', *fighting.*

Castle Forbes siege—Attempt in Paris to assassinate Sir Adam Gordon by a Forbes—View from Mar road—Gadie.

ineffectual siege the Gordons abandoned their attack upon the Castle, and proceeded northwards, having, in the death of Black Arthur, struck a mortal blow at the power of the rival clan.

The bitterness, however, of feudal revenge survived, and some of the Forbes family determined to avenge Black Arthur's death upon the opposite leader, Sir Adam Gordon. Sir Adam having gone to Paris with several gentlemen of his suite was received with great distinction by the French king (Charles). The Archbishop of Glasgow was then ambassador from Scotland to the court of France, and invited Sir Adam and his friends to a splendid supper. On his return from the Archbishop's hotel to his lodging about midnight, he and his train were set upon by armed men, and it was only after a severe struggle in which Sir Adam received a shot through the knee that the assassins were put to flight. In the pursuit, one of them dropped his hat, which being picked up appeared to have belonged to one of the name of Forbes. Inquiries having been set on foot, the whole conspiracy was traced, and the leaders of it put to the rack, and executed.

The Mar road passing by Knockespock is a green turf road in the midst of the heather, winding along the side of the hills to Kildrummie, affording along the whole way very pleasing views of a large portion of the Garioch, Strathbogie, and Mar, the Tap of Noth, the Buck of the Cabrach, Huntly Castle, Drumminor, Craig, Leith Hall, Gordon Hall (otherwise Wardhouse), Clova, Glenbogie, the rivers Gadie and Bogie.

(*o*) Gadie, see " The Wedded Waters," p. 142, 143.

INDEX OF PERSONS AND PLACES.

Aberdeen, City of Old, 147, 148
   ,,   Bishops of, 173
   ,,   Cathedral of, 71.175
   ,,   Diocese of, 116
   ,,   City of New, 7.39.43. 46. 51. 68, 69, 70. 84. 91. 111. 116, 117. 179
   ,,   Herald, 40. 53. 164
   ,,   Journal, 41
   ,,   Infirmary, 136
   ,,   School of Industry, 155
   ,,   Shire of, 39. 108. 175, 176, 178. 180
Aberdeen, Earl of, 116
Abernethy, Sir Wm., 69
Adam, Jas., Esq., 40. 86
Alcluid (Glasgow, on the Clyde?) 177
Aldivalloch, 175. 181
Alford, 147
Allen, 26
America, 21
Anderson, Lieut.-Gen. Andrew, 79, 80
Angus, 68, 69
   ,,   Earl of, 180
Annie, 64
Aoth, King, 98
Argyle, Marquess of, 174

Ariosto, 176, 178
Arthur, Black, of Forbes, 170. 179. 183, 184
   ,,   King, 177
Auchindoir, 182
Auchindoun, Sir Adam Gordon of, 173. 183
Ayrshire, 174

Badenoch, 180
   ,,   Wolf of, 77
Balgounie, Bridge of, 147, 148
Balguay, 24, 26
Balquhain, 67. 69. 71
Balquhidder, Braes of, 14
Banff, Sheriffdom of, 148
Bass of Inverury, 98. 147
Belmont-street, Aberdeen, 7
Benachie, 58, 59. 70. 98. 104. 125, 126. 133. 143. 148. 168. 173. 175
Ben Nevis, 180
Berwick-on-Tweed, 176
Birnam Wood, 85
Blackstone, Judge, 56
Boccania (*see* Buchan)
Bogie, 170. 177. 179. 182. 184
Bohemia, 116
Bon Accord, 175
Bruce, King Robert, 74. 147. 176. 179

Bruce's Queen, 176
„ Nigel, 176
Buchan, 69. 178
„ Earl of, 178
„ Constable of France, 175
„ Logie of, 175
Bucket, 147
Burleigh House, 180
Burns (Poet), 174
Burnes, 174
Byron, Lord, 13. 147. 175

Cabrach, 170. 181, 182. 184
Cabria (*see* Cabrach)
Cairelegion (Caerleon), 177
Calcutta, 191
Caledonia, 18
Cameron, 110
Cardin Brig and Muir, 65
Carlisle, 177
Cauld Kail in Aberdeen (Song), 179
Ceres, 73
Chalmers, 42
Chambers, Robert, 21
Chantrey, Sir Francis, 52
Charlemagne, 176
Charles I., King, 116
„ King of France, 184
Charles Edward, Prince, 174
Cheyne, Bishop, 147
Cheynes of Essilmont, 115
Clatt, Barony of, 173
„ Parish of, 143. 173, 174
Clochnabin, 175
Clova, 184
Cochrane, 173
Constantinople, 71
Cooper, John, 27

Cornwaile, 177
Corrichie, 71
Craig, House of, 181, 182. 184
Craigievar, 174, 180
Craigphatrie, 177
Cromwell Park, 32
Cults, 116
Cummin, 180
Cunningham, Allan, 52. 174
Cupar-Angus, 21
Cyprus, 55

David II., King, 71. 178
Davidson, Sir Robert, 69
Dee, 98
Deveron, 179
Don, 54. 68, 69. 98. 123. 147, 148. 176
Donald of the Isles, 68
„ Tomb of, 70
Donnydowre (*see* Dunnideer)
Dooley, Lieut., 162, 164
Douglas, Earl of, 71. 178
Dover, 177
Drum, 69. 71
Drumdurno, 59, 60
Drumminor, 170. 175, 176. 179. 183, 184
Drummond (of Hawthornden), 69
Dumfermling, 116
Dumfries, 174. 180
Dumourier, 74
Dunbar, 178
Dunbritayn (Dumbarton), 177
Dundee, 21. 23. 110
„ Constable of, 68, 69
Dunfirse (Dumfries), 178, 179
Dunnideer, 170. 174. 177, 178
Dunsinane, 85

INDEX OF PERSONS AND PLACES.

Eachin Rusidh ni Cath, 71
East Indies, 79
Edinburgh, 48. 116. 118. 174. 177
Edward I., King, 176
Elgin, 78. 80
    „   Cathedral of, 77
Elizabeth Thom (*see* Thom)
Elphinstone, Sir Robert Horne Dalrymple, Bart., of Logie, 47
England, 52. 166. 180
Eoth, 98
Errol, 29, 30. 32
Erskines, Earls of Mar, 177, 178
Essilmont, 115
    „   Cheynes of, 115
    „   Miss Gordon of, 115
Ettrick Shepherd, 14

Fetterneir, 67, 68, 69. 71
Findonness, 164
Firth of Forth, 164
Flodden, 173
Footdee, 163
Forbes, 71. 170. 175, 176. 178, 179. 183, 184
    „   Castle of, 175. 179. 183, 184
Forgue, 115
Forfarshire, 5. 21
Foundland Hill, 115
France, 180. 184

Gadie, 58. 98. 143. 148. 171. 175. 184
Garioch, 39. 54. 58. 175. 184.
    „   Chapel of, 69
Gartly, Castle of, 148

German Ocean, 148
Gillespie, Elspet, 84, 85
Gilzean, Marjory (Gillan), 78
Glasgow, Archbishop of, 184
Glenbogie, 184
Glenbucket, 147
Glendinning, Matthew Sharpe, 174
Gleneifer, 14
Goldsmith, 34
Gordon's Hospital, Aberdeen 13
Gordon Hall, 184
Gordon, Robert, of Straloch, 148
    „   „   of Craig, 182
    „   Miss, of Essilmont, 115
    „   Bruce's friend, 180
    „   of Pitlurg, 180
    „   Sir Adam, of Auchindoun, 173. 183, 184
Gordoun, George, First Marquess of Huntly, 181
    „   Alexander, Duke of, 177. 179
    „   Col. Charles, R. A., 176
Gordon, Barron and Co., 46. 50
Gordon, Clan, 170. 176. 179. 183, 184
Gowrie, Carse of, 24. 30. 32
Grant, Clan, 181
Grant, Foulerton, 176
Gregory, King, 177

Hardyng, Jhon, Chronicle, 177
Harlaw, 59. 68, 69, 70, 71. 98
Harthill, 168. 174, 175

Hatfield House, 180
Hawthornden, 70. 115
Hector Rufus Bellicosus, 71
Heidelberg, 180
Highland Harry, 173
Highland Distillery Line, 174
Holland, 74
Homer, 34
Huntingtower, 32
Huntly, Earl of, 71. 180. 183
  ,, Marquess of, 181
  ,, Marquise of, 181
  ,, Castle of, 170. 179. 184

Inchmartin, 26
Inchture, 24
Inverness, 70. 114. 177
Invernochty, 147
Inverury, 3. 39. 43. 47. 54. 68. 70. 74. 98. 110. 133. 134. 136. 148. 152. 154. 174, 175
Irvine's, 68
  ,, Sir Alexander of Drum, 69. 71
Isles, Lord of the, 70

James I. of England, 173
  ,, IV. of Scotland, do. 173
  ,, VI. ,, do. 173. 183
  ,, VIII. ,, do. 178
Jamie, 112. 131, 132.
Jean, 58
Jessie, 93, 94
Johnston, Arthur, 182

Kearn, 176
Keig, 176
Kelly, 115

Kildrummie, 170. 176, 177, 178. 184
Kinnaird, 24. 27, 28
Kintore, Lass of, 123, 124
Knockespock, James Gordoun 173
  ,, George, 168, 169. 171, 172
  ,, Jean Leith, (Knockespock's Lady,) 169. 172
  ,, James Adam Gordon, 27. 41. 42. 44, 45. 49, 50. 52. 173
  ,, Emma Katherine, Dedication to, 52
  ,, Water, Marches, &c. 173. 176
  ,, Place, 173, 174. 177 168, 183, 184

Lauchlan Lubanich, 71
Lauriston, 69
Leith, (Town) 79. 164
Leiths, 168. 174
Leith Hall, 184
Leopold I. Emperor, 71
Leslies of Balquhain, 71
  ,, Walter, 71
  ,, John, 71
  ,, Count, 67, 68. 70
Leslie, Andrew, 69
Leslie's Cross, 69
Lesley, General David, 174
Lochaber, 180
Lochnagar, 175
Logie o' Buchan, 175
  ,, Elphinstone, 65. 142, 143

INDEX OF PERSONS AND PLACES.

London, 21. 51, 52. 79. 116. 133. 174
Lovels, 68
„ James, 69
Lumphanan, 176
Lumsden, Harry, 173, 174

Macbeth, 176
Macdonald, 71
Macfarlane's Collections, 70
Macintosh clan, 181
Macintosh, 68, 69, 70
Maclean, 68, 69, 70
Macnaghten, 50
Maiden Stone, 61
Malvern Water, 173
Mar, 39. 170. 178. 184
Mar, Earls of, 68, 69, 70. 176 178
Mar's Road, 170. 177. 184
Marmion, 180
Mary, 91, 92. 96
Mary, Queen of Scots, 71, 183
Maules, The, 68
Maule, Sir Robert, 69
Mearns, 68, 69
Meggy, 153
Menzies, Sir Thos., of Cults, 116
Methlick, 115
Methven, 33, 34, 35
Mill of Tiftie's Annie, 175
Mirimachi, 18
Montrose, Marquess of, 175
Moneymusk, 175
Moore, Thomas (Anacreon) 13
Morayshire, 77. 178
Mortimer, Isabel, 69
Murith (*see* Morayshire)
Murrays, The, 68

Murray, Earl of, Regent, 178
Murray, Sir Thomas, 69
Nairn, 72
Naish House, 166
Newton, by Old Rayne, 98
Newtyle, 5. 21, 22
New York, 191
Niel Gow, 16
Nigel, Bruce, 176
Nochty, 147
Northumberland, 144
Noth, Tap of, 170. 176, 177. 184

Ogilvie, Sir Alexander, 69
„ George, 69
Old Rayne, 98
Orlando Furioso, 175. 178
Ottley, Lucy Lawrence, 166

Paesenneock, 173
Paisley, 118
Panmure, 69
Paris, 184
Paphos, 55
Parnassus, 18
"Peasant, worthy," name unknown, 27
Peggy of Kintore, 124
Perth, 32, 177
Peterhead, 108
Pictish Houses, 177
Pitlurg, Chief of Gordon Clan, 180
Pitmachie, 51
Pittodrie, 58, 59, 60, 61
Playfair, 24
Putachie, 176
Ravenscraig Castle, 108
Rhynie, 176. 179

Richmond, Duke of, 177
Rithemay, 177
Robertson, J., Esq., 133
Ross, Earl of, 70
Round Table, 177
Roy's wife, 181

Salisbury, Earl of, 176
Saltoun, 69
Saracens, 176
Sclavonia, 71
Scotland, 52. 57. 69. 98. 115, 116, 117, 118. 140. 177. 180. 183, 184.
Scott's, Sir Walter, Tales of a Grandfather, 181
Scrymgeour, Sir James, 68, 69
Shelley, 108. 121
Spalding Club, 116.
Steuart, Henrietta, 181
St. Johnstoune, 178
Stirling, Alexander, 69
Stirlings, 68
Stocks, 93
Straiton, 68
    „   Sir Alexander, 69
Straloch, Robt. Gordon of, 148
Strathbogie, 39. 177. 179. 184
Strathdon, 147
Striveline (Stirling), 177
Stuart, James, Earl of Murray, 178
Suie Hill, 173
Surgundo Poem, 173

Tannahill, poet and weaver, 14
Tantallon Castle, 180
Tay, 97, 98
Thinclaith, Bailie, 159
Thom, William, 50, 51

Thom, Jean or Jeanie, 36. 97. 133. 138
  „ Jeanie, 25. 27, 28
  „ William, or Willie, 25. 47. 51. 133, 134, 135, 136. 139
  „ Elizabeth, or Betsy, 47. 51. 133, 134
  „ James, or Jamie, 47. 51
Thomas the Rhymer, 98
Thompson, Dr., of Inverury, 50
Tillyangus, 170. 179. 181. 183
Tours, Castle of, 180
Tring, 93
Tytler, 70
Tweed, 98

Ugie, 108
Ury, 54. 57, 58. 68. 70. 97, 98. 121, 122, 123. 143, 147, 148

Venus, 55
Vienna, 71
Volney, 9
Wallace, 71
  „ Tower, 71
Wallenstein, Count, 71
Wardhouse, or Wardes, 174. 176. 184
Waverley, 13
Weekly Chronicle, 48, 49
Willie, the Porter, 91

Ythan, 115
Ythanside, 114, 115

THE AUTHOR'S ACKNOWLEDGMENT.

In taking leave of my readers for a time—I trust we may meet again—I would just like to allude to certain matters resulting from the First Edition of this little book. For its success, and the good things that followed, my prime thanks are due to the Public Press: It, with little exception, exhibited the best portions of my book, with the best effect. Above all, they found in my narrative and song a text from which they worked a powerful and enduring sympathy towards the Trade-stricken, whose sorrows and shiftings are but too feebly told in my own experiences.

That same is no mean reward.

A selfish and personal pity *was never sought for by me*,—nor had I a single wish all the while beyond the utterance of my private feelings, and the pleasure such utterance affords to a stifled and unregarded suffering. I made *no* appeal. Yet there have arisen many friends willing to see me above the chances of again tasting the evils I attempted to describe. From these friends I have received a sufficiency to make good a beginning,—

enough, with ordinary prudence, to carry me and mine safely onwards. The details of what I merely now hint at, are well recorded, and will be spoken of another time. But now Pride alone (Gratitude unmentioned) urges me, on the instant, to acknowledge handsome donations, from my countrymen and others, in New York and Calcutta, accompanied by kind and earnest expressions of regard. These sums are now invested for the future good of my three children. Whatever else we possess will be applied, with our best industry, for our common happiness.

June 4th, 1845.

WILLIAM THOM

January, 1848.

CATALOGUE
OF
SMITH, ELDER AND CO.'S PUBLICATIONS.

WORKS IN THE PRESS.

SIR THEODORE BROUGHTON; or, LAUREL WATER.

A Romance. By G. P. R. JAMES, Esq. Author of "The Convict," "Russell," "Ehrenstein," &c. &c. (*Early in April.*)

ADVENTURES OF AN AIDE-DE-CAMP:

Or, A CAMPAIGN IN CALABRIA. By JAMES GRANT, Esq. Author of "The Romance of War; or, the Highlanders in Spain." 3 vols. post 8vo. (*Just ready.*)

THE PRACTICAL SUGAR PLANTER:

A COMPLETE ACCOUNT OF THE CULTIVATION AND MANUFACTURE OF THE SUGAR-CANE, according to the latest and most improved processes; describing and comparing the different Systems pursued in the East and West Indies, and the Straits of Malacca, and the relative expenses and advantages attendant upon each: being the result of Sixteen Years actual experience as a Sugar Planter in those Countries. By LEONARD WRAY, Esq. One vol. 8vo., with numerous Illustrations. (*Nearly ready.*)

THE PATRIARCHS—THE PROPHETS—THE APOSTLES.

Their characters and influence on the ages in which they lived, considered in counexion with the Christian Dispensation. By the Rev. GEORGE CROLY, LL.D. To form a series of three separate and independent volumes.

The First Volume, treating of the PATRIARCHS, will shortly appear.

ENGLISH EPITHETS, NATURAL AND FIGURATIVE:

With ELEMENTARY REMARKS, and MINUTE REFERENCES TO ABUNDANT AUTHORITIES. In one vol. imperial 8vo. (*Nearly ready.*)

Preparing for Publication, by the same Author,

THE ENGLISH GRADUS.
TO APPEAR IN PARTS.

A Prospectus and Specimen will shortly be issued.

MR. LEIGH HUNT'S GIFT BOOK.

A JAR OF HONEY FROM MOUNT HYBLA.

By LEIGH HUNT. Illustrated by RICHARD DOYLE. Square demy 8vo, in a novel and elegant binding, price 14s.

"A jar of honey!—the announcement is seasonable. There is a promise of enjoyment in the very shape of the vessel—to say nothing of the graceful devices with which it is in this instance adorned. Not only does it contain a genuine sweetness, but it is wreathed, so to speak, with the flowers from which that sweetness has been derived. The volume includes a retrospect of the mythology, history, and biography of Sicily, ancient legends, examples of pastoral poetry selected from Greece, Italy, and Britain; illustrative criticisms on these topics, and pleasant discursions on others which are collateral. These are prefaced by a genial introduction. It is a book acceptable at all seasons. Its value is enhanced by the graceful fancy displayed in Mr. Doyle's illustrations; and amongst the books which suggest themselves as the best of gifts in a season of gifts, we know none that more gracefully recommends itself than 'The Jar of Honey.'"—*Athenæum*.

"A luxury of taste pervades the illustration, the printing, even the binding. The jar is filled with delicate and noble fancies; with genuine Christmas associations of 'poetry, piety, revelry, superstition, story-telling, and masquing;' with pastoral and fire-side thoughts, and thoughts of deep humanity; with Fairy tales of antiquity, and the gossip of ancient holidays, and the Christmas poetry and cheerful piety of old. Everything is turned to pleasurable account."—*Examiner*.

"The title of this collection of pastoral and poetical fireside talk gives us a hint of the suggestive character of the contents. Out of a chaos of sweet fancies and high thoughts springs this elegant volume—the work of a poet and civiliser, who has done more in his time to multiply the springs of intellectual and social pleasure than most of his contemporaries. The binding and illustrations deserve a word of admiration—the cover for its quaintness and appropriateness, and the designs for their delicacy and poetical spirit. The volume is abundantly rich in claims of every kind."—*Atlas*.

"This is by far the most beautiful gift-book of the season. This Sicilian and Cerulean jar is full of honey, which in its sweetness never cloys. Leigh Hunt has learned on Hybla a new chemistry, and has imparted to this vase a power to preserve its purity and sweetness, while it imbibes a spirit and a flavour as healthful and as varied as the most fastidious and exacting taste can require."—*Tablet*.

"Mr. Leigh Hunt's 'Jar of Honey from Mount Hybla' is just one of those gossiping, kindly things that emanate from this author's pen, showing reading of the works of all sorts of poets, ancient and modern, English and foreign, and a disposition to quote them right heartily. There is a revelling in the stores of poetical literature, an aptness in chasing a thyme from poet to poet, a luxuriance of quotation, which marks the rambling prose papers of Mr. Hunt from the days of the *Indicator* downwards. The cover itself is promising, with the blue jar standing in such commanding relief among the flowers and leaves that are gilt and illuminated around it."—*Times*.

"As a pleasant and very various melange, touching upon mythology, poetry, history, customs, tales of life, and sketches of nature, opposite to each other as a flood of lava and a purling stream, 'A Jar of Honey' is just the thing for the season—pretty to look at, a something to pass about from hand to hand, full of pointed specimens to be read in a minute or two, and so divided that the book may be laid down at any time. The main composition is full of penetrating remarks cleverly expressed: Addison's definition of fine writing—thoughts natural but not obvious."—*Spectator*.

"The author of this work is fully justified in designating it 'A Christmas Book.' It is one of the very best we have ever read, for it has a sound practical moral attached to it. It is the very book to be placed in the hands of boys at this season; for, whilst it amuses and delights them, it is particularly well calculated to give them a taste for classical literature—to make them relish at the fireside at home that which has been so harsh and so unpleasant in the school-room. It induces a love for classical literature. Most justly does Leigh Hunt designate his work 'A Jar of Honey;' for within its narrow compass will be found compressed the very aroma of many a day's reading, many a night's study, and many an hour's intense thought. It is a charming book, full of delicate fancies."—*Morning Herald*.

"This beautiful volume is the graceful result of extended reading and elegant taste. As a work suggestive of fine literature, pure morals, and good feeling, it may take rank with the best productions of its class in the entire range of English compilation."—*Observer*.

MR. LEIGH HUNT'S ESSAYS.

MEN, WOMEN, AND BOOKS:

A Selection from his hitherto Uncollected Prose Writings. By Leigh Hunt. In two vols. post 8vo., with a Portrait of the Author by Severn.

CONTENTS.

Vol. I.
- Fiction and Matter of Fact.
- Inside of an Omnibus.
- The Day of the Disasters of Carfington Blundell, Esq.
- A Visit to the Zoological Gardens.
- A Man introduced to his Ancestors.
- A Novel Party.
- Beds and Bedrooms.
- The World of Books.
- Jack Abbott's Breakfast.
- On seeing a Pigeon make Love.
- The Month of May.
- The Guili Tre.
- A Few Remarks on the Rare Vice called "Lying."
- Criticism on Female Beauty.
- On deceased Statesmen who have written Verses.
- Female Sovereigns of England.

Vol. II.
- Social Morality—Suckling and Ben Jonson.
- Pope in some lights in which he is not usually regarded.
- Garth, Physicians, and Love-Letters.
- Cowley and Thomson.
- Bookstalls and "Galateo."
- Bookbinding and "Heliodorus."
- Ver-Vert; or, the Parrot of the Nuns.
- Duchess of St. Albans; and Marriages from the Stage.
- Specimens of British Poetesses.
- Life and Writings of Lady Mary Wortley Montagu.
- Life and African Journey of Pepys.
- Life and Letters of Madame de Sevigne.

"The sketches before us have durable characteristics. They are full of variety, beauty, and cheerfulness. This is a book to be in the cherished corner of a pleasant room and to be taken up when the spirits have need of sunshine. The book which the present most resembles in Mr. Hunt's former writings (and this is a great compliment) is the *Indicator*. Its papers have the same cordial mixture of fact and imagination."—*Examiner*.

"Mr. Leigh Hunt never writes otherwise than cheerfully. He *will* have sunshine---*will* promote gay spirits---*will* uphold liberal truths; blithely, yet earnestly. He is the Prince of Parlour-window writers."—*Athenæum*.

"A book for a parlour-window, for a summer's eve, for a warm fireside, for a half-hour's leisure, for a whole day's luxury---in any and every possible shape a charming companion."—*Westminster Review*.

"There is much variety and agreeable lore of all kinds in these volumes; a soul of reflection, brilliant animal spirits, and a cheerful philosophy. The subjects embrace almost every topic of a pleasurable and a refining kind."—*Atlas*.

"Papers illustrative of social matters, comicalities, and jovialities, arising from fine spirits and delicate perceptions, light and elegant criticisms, and dissertations on beauties, floral and feminine; all abounding with that suggestive power which marks the long course of this author's writings."—*Jerrold's Newspaper*.

"Here we have grouped together the raciest of the papers which Leigh Hunt wrote in the palmiest days of his literary strength, when his wit was two-edged, and his humour richest, merriest, most hilarious, running over into lavish abundance of conceits, and occasionally as boisterous as the veriest group in the playgrounds."—*Atlas*.

FIRST WORK OF A NEW NOVELIST.

JANE EYRE; AN AUTOBIOGRAPHY.

By CURRER BELL. Second Edition, with Preface by the Author. 3 vols. post 8vo, price £1 11s. 6d. cloth.

"A book of decided power. The thoughts are true, sound, and original: and the style is resolute, straightforward, and to the purpose. The object and moral of the work are excellent. Without being professedly didactic, the writer's intention (amongst other things) seems to be, to show how intellect and unswerving integrity may win their way, although oppressed by that predominating influence in society which is a mere consequence of the accidents of birth or fortune. In the end, the honesty, kindness of heart, and perseverance of the heroine, are seen triumphant over every obstacle. As an analysis of a single mind, as an elucidation of its progress from childhood to full age, it may claim comparison with any work of the same species."—*Examiner*.

"Almost all that we require in a novelist the writer has: perception of character and power of delineating it; picturesqueness, passion, and knowledge of life. The story is not only of singular interest, naturally evolved, unflagging to the last, but it fastens itself upon your attention, and will not leave you. The book closed, the enchantment continues: your interest does not cease. Reality—deep, significant reality, is the characteristic of this book."—*Fraser's Magazine*.

"The most extraordinary production that has issued from the press for years. We know no author who possesses such power as is exhibited in these three volumes. No writer who can sustain such a calm, mental tone, and so deeply interest without having recourse to any startling expedients. From the first page to the last, it is stamped with vitality."—*Weekly Chronicle*.

"One of the most powerful domestic romances which have been published for many years; full of youthful vigour, of freshness and originality, of nervous diction, and concentrated interest. It is a book to make the pulses gallop and the heart beat, and to fill the eyes with tears. It is a book with a great heart in it."—*Atlas*.

"Of all the novels we have read for years this is the most striking, and we may add, the most interesting. Its style as well as its characters are unhackneyed, perfectly fresh and life-like. It is thoroughly English. The story is artistically managed, the characters boldly and vigorously drawn, and the whole calculated to interest and enchain the reader."—*Economist*.

"The autobiography of 'Jane Eyre' is simply the development of a human mind: the growth, the strength, the restraint, direction, and subduing; the education and guidance, under formation, of a powerful intellect prompted by a strong will. The thread of the story is strung with pearls—pearls of thought and sentiment, and it winds round the reason and the affections. The reading of such a book as this is a healthful exercise."—*Tablet*.

"Original, vigorous, edifying, and absorbingly interesting.---*Jerrold's Newspaper*.

"The characters introduced are strongly marked; the incidents are various, and of a kind which enlist the sympathies: the style is fresh and vigorous, and thrilling interest is excited."---*Morning Post*.

"An extraordinary book of its kind, and as truly of a most noble purpose, considerable originality, and high promise. It will be read by most people with pleasure, and laid down by all with regret."—*Observer*.

"The fiction belongs to that school where minute anatomy of the mind predominates over incidents; the last being made subordinate to description or the display of character. The book displays considerable skill in the plan, and great power."—*Spectator*.

"For power of thought and expression we do not know its rival among modern productions. The tale is one of the heart, and the working out of a moral through the natural affections; it is the victory of mind over matter; the mastery of reason over feeling, without unnatural sacrifices. The story itself is unique. There is much to ponder over, rejoice over, and weep over, in its ably written pages."---*Era*.

"One of the freshest and most genuine books which we have read for a long time. It is a domestic story, full of the most intense interest, and yet composed of the simplest materials, the worth of which consists in their truth."---*Howitt's Journal*.

"This is one of the most notable domestic novels which have issued from the press for many years past. The style is bold, lucid, pungent; the incidents are varied, touching, romantic; the characterisation is ample, original, diversified: the moral sentiments are pure and healthy; and the whole work is calculated to rivet attention, to provoke sympathy, to make the heart bound and the brain pause."---*People's Journal*.

MR. G. P. R. JAMES'S LAST NOVEL.

THE CONVICT.

A Tale. By G. P. R. James, Esq. Three vols. post 8vo., price £1 11s. 6d.

"The volumes are well filled with incident; the sentiments are those of a reflective and well-constituted mind; there is a perpetual flow of invention in the conduct of the story; and it agreeably combines a spirit of romance with a just delineation of social life and manners."—*Britannia*.

"That novel reader must have an exorbitant appetite, who should complain of want of variety in this tale. It is crush-full of incidents, and presents changes of scene which bring the antipodes together. It is studded with effects, and has enough materials for at least a couple of ordinary novels."—*Atlas*.

"The plot is cleverly contrived, so as to arrest the attention of the reader unflaggingly, and to introduce a great variety of scenery, incident, and character. All the points of this excellently told tale are managed with a skilful hand. It is stirring, entertaining, and oftentimes affecting; and there are scenes, thoughts, descriptions, and traits of character, which, while they amuse, are valuable from their suggestive, elevating, and purifying tendency."—*Morning Advertiser*.

A WHIM AND ITS CONSEQUENCES.

In three vols. post 8vo., price £1 11s. 6d.

"Full of talent, equal to the most touching pictures of human life, and descriptions of rich scenery—to the development of character, and to those minute touches of the pencil which prove great acuteness of observation, and a peculiar tact in illuminating a whole subject by a brilliant stroke of nature and art."—*Literary Gazette*.

"One of the most brilliant fictions the season has produced. The author's style is singularly vigorous and graphic. Whether he attempts humour or pathos, the author is equally happy in rousing the sympathies of his readers."—*Critic*.

"The story is worked out with such remarkable dramatic powers as fairly to fascinate the reader. It is a perfect piece of legal romance."—*Atlas*.

HARDEN HALL; or, THREE PROPOSALS.

Edited by the Hon. F—— B——. Three vols. post 8vo., price £1 11s. 6d.

"The writer appears to be well acquainted with the circles he describes. The leading characters are drawn with considerable force and skill."—*Literary Gazette*.

"A very pleasantly written, amusing, cleverly conducted, fashionable novel. The chief persons of the story are strongly conceived, ably pourtrayed, and preserved in excellent keeping throughout. The scenes of fashionable life, too, are sketched with more than usual vividness of style."—*Naval and Military Gazette*.

LECTURES ON THE HISTORY AND PRINCIPLES OF ANCIENT COMMERCE.

By J. W. Gilbart, Esq. F.R.S. Post 8vo, price 7s. 6d. cloth.

"Full of practical intelligence and sound reasoning."—*Literary Gazette*.

"An able and very readable compendium."—*Spectator*.

"A work useful to students of political economy, and interesting to the general reader."—*Economist*.

"Mr. Gilbart writes forcibly and well, and has collected together a mass of useful information, well digested and lucidly arranged."—*Morning Post*.

"This volume contains much valuable information, rendered more interesting by a wise deduction of sound principles."—*Jerrold's Newspaper*.

QUESTIONS AND ANSWERS:

Suggested by a Consideration of some of the Arrangements and Relations of Social Life; being a Sequel to the "Outlines of Social Economy," by the same Author. Foolscap 8vo. price 2s. 6d. half-bound.

"The author of these various manuals of the social sciences has the art of stating clearly the abstruse points of political economy and metaphysics, and making them level to every understanding. His book gives a fair, concise, and clear view of all the important questions of political economy, and is admirably well calculated to introduce students to more formal works."—*Economist.*

VIEWS OF KOT KANGRA.

Representing the Passage of the British Force under Brigadier Wheeler, C.B., to whom the Fortress surrendered; with Portrait of Soondur Singh, Killadar of the Fort. Coloured facsimiles of six original drawings made on the Spot by Lieut.-Col. JACK, 80th Regt. N.I., with Descriptions. Colombier, in a Portfolio. Price Two Guineas.

SERMONS,

Preached at the FOUNDLING HOSPITAL; with others preached in ST. STEPHEN'S, Walbrook. By the Rev. GEORGE CROLY, LL.D. One vol. 8vo, price 10s. 6d. cloth.

THE HAMPDEN CONTROVERSY.

A CONCISE HISTORY OF THE HAMPDEN CONTROVERSY, from the Commencement in 1832 to the present time. With Extracts showing the tendency of the Bampton Lectures delivered by Dr. HAMPDEN, and Copies of all the Documents that have appeared on the subject. By the Rev. HENRY CHRISTMAS, M.A., F.R.S., F.S.A., &c. &c. 8vo. price 4s. 6d. boards.

SCRIPTURAL EPITAPHS.

A SELECTION OF PASSAGES FROM SCRIPTURE SUITABLE FOR CHRISTIAN EPITAPHS. Price 2s. 6d. cloth lettered. An edition on large paper, price 4s. cloth.

"This is a highly useful and much wanted work, bringing into one view all the passages in Holy Writ that can be deemed applicable to the faith and hope of departed spirits, or the love of the survivors. The inscriptions are all brief, and most judiciously selected."—*Nottingham Mercury.*

"The work is appropriately 'got up,' each page representing a monumental slab, the Epitaphs being printed in black letter."—*Bath Herald.*

REASON, REVELATION, AND FAITH:

SOME FEW THOUGHTS BY A BENGAL CIVILIAN. 12mo, price 5s. cloth.

June, 1847.

CATALOGUE

OF

SMITH, ELDER AND CO.'S PUBLICATIONS.

WORKS IN THE PRESS.

THE REV. DR. CROLY.

THE PATRIARCHS—THE PROPHETS—THE APOSTLES.
Their characters and influence on the ages in which they lived, considered in connexion with the Christian dispensation. To form a series of three separate and independent volumes.

The First Volume, treating of the PATRIARCHS, will shortly appear.

MR. LEIGH HUNT.

A JAR OF HONEY FROM MOUNT HYBLA.
By LEIGH HUNT. With Illustrations by RICHARD, JAMES, and HENRY DOYLE. One vol. elegantly bound.

MR. ANDREW STEINMETZ.

JESUITISM PORTRAYED:
Or, THE INFLUENCE OF THE JESUITS ON MANKIND, as shewn by their "Constitutions," History, Missions, and the Characters and Power of the "Generals" of the Society. By ANDREW STEINMITZ. One vol. post 8vo.

MR. G. P. R. JAMES.

RUSSELL: A TALE OF THE RYE-HOUSE PLOT.
By G. P. R. JAMES, Esq. 3 vols. post 8vo. *(Just ready.)*

THE SURRENDER OF KOT KANGRA.

SIX VIEWS OF KOT KANGRA, AND THE SURROUNDING COUNTRY.
Representing the Passage of the British Force under Brigadier Wheeler, C.B., to whom the Fortress surrendered. With Portrait of Loondur Singh, Killedar of the Fort. Coloured facsimiles of the original drawings made on the spot by Lieut.-Col. JACK, 30th Regt. N. I. with Descriptions. Colombier Folio.

New Publications.

MR. LEIGH HUNT'S NEW WORK.
MEN, WOMEN, AND BOOKS:

Being a SELECTION OF SKETCHES, ESSAYS, and CRITICAL MEMOIRS, from his uncollected Prose Writings. By LEIGH HUNT. 2 vols. post 8vo., with Portrait of the Author, price One Guinea, cloth.

A ROMANCE OF THE PRESENT DAY.
A WHIM AND ITS CONSEQUENCES.

In 3 vols. post 8vo. price 1l. 11s. 6d.

"Full of talent, equal to the most touching pictures of human life, and descriptions of rural scenery — to the development of character, and to those minute touches of the pencil which prove great acuteness of observation, and a peculiar tact in illuminating a whole subject by a brilliant stroke of nature and art. The author displays sound sense on grave topics, affecting sentiment on human vicissitudes and sorrows, quiet humour on subjects susceptible of playful illustrations and simplicity combined. We welcome him as a very smart and able accession to the scanty roll of our successful living novelists."—*Literary Gazette*.

"One of the most brilliant fictions the season has produced. The author's style is singularly vigorous and graphic. Whether he attempts humour or pathos, the author is equally happy in rousing the sympathies of his readers."—*Critic*.

"The story is worked out with such remarkable dramatic powers as fairly to fascinate the reader. It is a perfect piece of legal romance."—*Atlas*.

"A clever novel of the old school. It is the story of an Orlando after Shakspeare's pattern. Whether by an old or a new hand, it deserves a good word for the earnestness with which it is written."—*Athenæum*.

"The story is very interesting, the characters are well and distinctly drawn, and the main occurrences powerfully described, while a remarkable shrewdness, causticity, and dry humour pervade the incidental observations on life and manners."—*Court Journal*.

AUTOBIOGRAPHY OF A NEGRO SLAVE.
THE LIFE AND ADVENTURES OF ZAMBA,

An Africa Negro King, and his experience of Slavery in South Carolina. Written by Himself. 1 vol. post 8vo. with Frontispiece, price 7s. 6d. cloth. Corrected and arranged by P. NEILSON.

"We have never read a more life-like book, or one in which there was a greater amount of truth-seeming. There is a simplicity about the style and incidents that is quite *Crusoish*."—*Weekly Chronicle*.

"We can conscientiously pronounce it to be a very well-written, interesting, and useful volume—useful, because it is another and severe blow levelled against the accursed stronghold of slavery; and we earnestly recommend its perusal to our readers."—*Weekly Dispatch*.

"It has a Robinson Crusoe sort of interest."—*Spectator*.

"The narrative has all the simplicity and strength of De Foe."—*Indian News*.

"A very interesting production. It is a plain, unvarnished tale, artless and unaffected, and carries conviction of its truth from its very simplicity."—*Journal of Fine Arts*.

"A curious production, and not without interest to the social and political student, as well as to the general reader. There is an air of natural simplicity about it not likely to be the result of artifice."—*Daily News*.

"Replete with deep interest. It is a genuine and interesting sketch of African domestic manners."—*New Monthly Magazine*.

"It bears internal evidence of truth. We think the book worth attention, because we regard it as essentially true."—*Britannia*.

"There is no want of interest in the story. The narrative is one which the reader, old or young, will not willingly throw aside."—*Atlas*.

LATEST ACCOUNT OF THE NEW ZEALANDERS.

SAVAGE LIFE AND SCENES IN AUSTRALIA AND NEW ZEALAND.

Being an Artist's impressions of Countries and People at the Antipodes. By GEORGE FRENCH ANGAS, Esq. Second edition, in two vols. post 8vo., with numerous Illustrations, price 24s. cloth.

"These volumes are the production of an intelligent and pains-taking traveller, who spent considerable time amongst the aborigines of Australia and of New Zealand, under circumstances peculiarly favourable to an accurate observation of their habits and character. Mr. Angas's volumes are enriched with numerous illustrations, and are eminently worthy of the confidence of readers. They bear the impress of truth, are the productions of an observant and intelligent mind, and will do more to familiarize our countrymen with the scenery and natives of the colonies described, than any other work with which we are acquainted."—*Eclectic Review.*

"The graphic style of the writing, and the high artistical character of the embellishments, bear out the description of these volumes in the title. The author has seen everything with an artist's eye, and recorded it with an artist's pen."—*Church of England Quarterly.*

"Mr. Angas writes as an artist; and he does not write the worse for that. We can see what he sees, because he understands the art of word-painting. All that he writes is eminently objective. There is an individuality in his descriptions which brings the scene or the person vividly before our eyes. It is nature—it is life—that is presented to us."—*Atlas.*

"Mr. Angas is just such an explorator, observer, and artist as we could wish to send out to any part of the world, civilised or uncivilised, of which we wished to have a fair description. Now Australia and New Zealand, of which so much has been written, are, as regards the pencil, almost undescribed countries, while they present, in the novel aspects of nature, much to interest, and as the field of colonization, appeal to deeper feelings than those of mere curiosity. * * The whole work is full of entertainment."—*Patriot.*

"Mr. Angas has evidently a passion for travelling, and nature has, in many ways, fitted him for this arduous pursuit. His style is joyous and readable, and we know not when we have read two volumes containing so much that is new and interesting."—*Jerrold's Magazine.*

"These are two volumes of good artistical description, with much of finer staple than the title-page promises. Mr. Angas observed nature in the Southern hemisphere with a painter's eye, and has thrown much poetical feeling into his impressions of it."—*Morning Chronicle.*

"He has not the bias or coarseness of many who have gone out to the antipodes; he has a better taste, in some sense a more cultivated mind, and is lifted above the atmosphere of Colonial partizanship."—*Spectator.*

"After a careful reading of these two volumes, we pronounce them, without any hesitation, to afford on the whole the most faithful pictures of savage life in Australia and New Zealand yet published."—*Weekly Chronicle.*

"Mr. Angas has happily shown the present state of the countries he has seen; and we will venture to say that his experience amongst the inhabitants of New Zealand extends further than that of any adventurer who may have preceded him."—*Douglas Jerrold's Weekly Newspaper.*

ACCOUNT OF THE ASSAMESE.

A SKETCH OF THE ASSAMESE.

With some Account of the Hill Tribes. By an OFFICER in the Hon. East India Company's Service. One vol. 8vo., with 16 Coloured Plates, a Map, and several Woodcuts, price 14s. cloth extra, or 20s. elegantly bound in calf.

MR. JAMES'S NEW NOVELS AND ROMANCES.

RUSSELL: A TALE OF THE RYE-HOUSE PLOT.

By G. P. R. James, Esq. 3 vols. post 8vo. (*Just ready.*)

THE CASTLE OF EHRENSTEIN:

Its Lords Spiritual and Temporal; its Inhabitants Earthly and Unearthly. By G. P. R. James, Esq. Author of "Heidelberg," "The Stepmother," "The Smuggler," &c. &c. In 3 vols. post 8vo. price 1*l*. 11*s*. 6*d*.

"This is undoubtedly one of the very best of Mr. James's Novels. The interest never flags throughout. It gives a most vivid picture of old German Chivalry."—*Weekly Chronicle.*

"We know not when we have been more—or indeed so much—gratified by the perusal of a work of fiction. It presents a great variety of well and strongly drawn characters. * * * We doubt whether Mr. James were ever more successful."—*Naval and Military Gazette.*

"This Romance is the best which its author has produced for a long time. It will prove very popular at the libraries."—*Critic.*

"We have a notion that this will prove the most permanently popular of all Mr. James's Novels, for it is compounded of those materials which delight all novel readers."—*John Bull.*

"Mr. James has laid the scene of this tale of the 15th century, on the banks of the Rhine. Admirable descriptions supply pictures of the period, such as the author can draw so well; he realizes the superstitions of that age, and fills the dreaded unknown as vividly as the actual and familiar of customary existence."—*Literary Gazette.*

HEIDELBERG:

A Romance. By G. P. R. James, Esq. Three vols. post 8vo. price 1*l*. 11*s*. 6*d*.

THE STEP-MOTHER.

By G. P. R. James, Esq. In 3 vols. post 8vo. price 1*l*. 11*s*. 6*d*.

ARRAH NEIL; or, TIMES OF OLD.

By G. P. R. James, Esq. Three vols. post 8vo. price 1*l*. 11*s*. 6*d*.

THE SMUGGLER.

A Novel. By G. P. R. James, Esq. Three vols. post 8vo. price 1*l*. 11*s*. 6*d*.

MR. JAMES'S CHARLEMAGNE.

THE HISTORY OF CHARLEMAGNE,

With a Sketch of the State and History of France, from the Fall of the Roman Empire to the Rise of the Carlovingian Dynasty. By G. P. R. James, Esq. A new edition, in demy 8vo. price 12*s*. cloth.

LEIGH HUNT'S SELECTIONS FROM THE ENGLISH POETS,
EXEMPLIFYING
I. IMAGINATION AND FANCY. II. WIT AND HUMOUR.
Bound in cloth, with gilt edges, price 10s. 6d. each.

Each volume is complete in itself, and preceded by an Essay illustrative of the qualities respectively exemplified in the selections; the best passages are marked and commented upon, and each author is characterized.

In "IMAGINATION AND FANCY," Mr. Leigh Hunt has given an answer to the question "What is Poetry?" in an Essay that forms an Introduction to the whole range of poetical invention; one region of which—the purely imaginative and fanciful—is investigated in a spirit of critical and genial enjoyment.

"WIT AND HUMOUR" is prefaced by an illustrative Essay, exemplifying the various modes in which these qualities have been manifested in Prose and Poetry.

Opinions of the Press on WIT AND HUMOUR.

"The design of this delightful series extends beyond a collection of elegant extracts, while it combines the best features of such collections. The two volumes already published are precisely the books one would wish to carry for companionship on a journey, or to have at hand when tired of work, or at a loss what to do for want of it. They are selections of some of the best things some of our best authors have said, accompanied with short but delicate expositions and enforcements of their beauties. They are truly most genial, agreeable, and social books."—*Examiner*.

"This is really a delightful volume, forming a proper complement and companion to its predecessor on 'Imagination and Fancy.' Each of them gives us the best passages of the best writers, in their respective kinds, illustrated by one who will himself leave no mean remembrance to posterity, in the spirit of genial criticism, informed by a delicate faculty of discrimination. What more could literary epicures desire?"—*Morning Chronicle*.

"If we were to choose the subject and the author of a fireside book for the long winter evenings, we should certainly call some such volume as this into existence. The reader will look for exquisite things in this book, and he will find a great deal more than he looks for in the prodigal resources opened up in its pages. It is the very essence of the sunniest qualities from English poets."—*Atlas*.

"There is something genial in the very title of this volume; and it does not belie its title. 'Wit and Humour,' forms a pendant to 'Imagination and Fancy,' by the same author. A like design is embodied in both works. The book is at once exhilarating and suggestive: it may charm frivolous minds into wisdom, and austere ones into mirth."—*Athenæum*.

Opinions of the Press on IMAGINATION AND FANCY.

"This volume is handsomely printed, and beautifully bound in a new style of exquisite delicacy and richness. In external beauty 'Imagination and Fancy' equals any gift-books that have appeared; and it will form a more enduring memorial than any other volume that might be selected as a gift for the coming season."—*Spectator*.

"This is a Christmas gift, worth half a dozen of the Annuals put together, and at half the cost of one of them. We have often wished for such a book, and in our aspiration, the name of Leigh Hunt has ever presented itself as that of the man above all others qualified to do justice to so charming a subject."—*Morning Chronicle*.

"The volume is, we trust, the precursor of many more, which will complete and do justice to the plan. The series so completed would be the best 'elegant extracts' in the language."—*Examiner*.

"This is a charming volume: both externally and internally it is most attractive."—*Atlas*.

"It is a book that every one who has a taste *must* have, and every one who has not *should* have in order to acquire one."—*Jerrold's Magazine*.

"This book is tastefully got up, and we should think better of the house where we saw a well-read copy of it lying about."—*Tait's Magazine*.

"These illustrations of 'Imagination and Fancy' are distinguished by great critical sagacity, and a remarkable appreciation of those qualities."—*Herald*.

The Third Volume of this Series, illustrative of
"ACTION AND PASSION,"
Will appear in the Autumn.

THE OXFORD GRADUATE ON ART.

"MODERN PAINTERS."

VOLUME THE FIRST. By A GRADUATE OF OXFORD. A New Edition, revised by the Author, being the THIRD. In imperial 8vo., price 18s. cloth.

SECOND VOLUME OF "MODERN PAINTERS."

Treating of the IMAGINATIVE and THEORETIC FACULTIES. By a GRADUATE OF OXFORD. In one volume, imperial 8vo., price 10s. 6d. cloth.

" We are prepared emphatically to declare, that this work is the most valuable contribution towards a proper view of painting, its purpose and means, that has come within our knowledge."—*Foreign Quarterly Review.*

" A work distinguished by an enlightened style of criticism, new to English readers, and by the profound observation of nature displayed by the author."—*Dublin University Magazine.*

" This is the production of a highly gifted mind, one who has evidently bestowed time and labour to obtain a practical knowledge of the fine arts, and who writes eloquently, feelingly, and fearlessly."—*Polytechnic Review.*

" It has seldom been our lot to take up a work more admirably conceived and written than this beautiful and elaborate essay. To a perfect idea of the scope of the inquiry, and a mastery of all the technicalities required for its due treatment, the Graduate unites considerable metaphysical power, extent of philosophical and scientific knowledge, a clear and manly style of expression, and no inconsiderable command of humour and satire."—*Atlas.*

" A very extraordinary and delightful book, full of truth and goodness, of power and beauty. This remarkable work contains more true philosophy,—more information of a strictly scientific kind,—more original thought and exact observation of nature,—more enlightened and serious enthusiasm, and more eloquent writing than it would be easy to match, not merely in works of its own class, but in those of any class whatever."—*North British Review.*

" A generous and impassioned review of the works of living painters: a hearty and earnest work, full of deep thought, and developing great and striking truths in art. The work, as a whole, commands our admiration. It lays before us the deeply studied reflections of a devout worshipper of nature—of one thoroughly imbued with the love of truth."—*British Quarterly Review.*

OUTLINES OF SOCIAL ECONOMY,

Written specially with a view to inculcate upon the rising generation the three great duties of Social Life:

1st. To strive to be self-supporting—not to be a burthen upon Society.

2nd. To avoid making any engagements, explicit or implied, whether with persons now living or yet to be born, for the due performance of which there is no reasonable prospect.

3rd. To make such use of all superior advantages, whether of knowledge, skill, or wealth, as to promote to the utmost the general happiness of mankind.

Foolscap 8vo., price 1s. 6d. half-bound.

⁎ The Publishers have instructions to supply to National Schools, British and Foreign Schools, and to all schools supported by Voluntary Contributions, a limited number of copies, at 6d. each.

OUTLINES OF THE HISTORY AND FORMATION OF THE UNDERSTANDING.

By the AUTHOR OF "OUTLINES OF SOCIAL ECONOMY." 1 vol. foolscap 8vo. price 2s. half bound.

THE JESUITS IN ENGLAND.

THE NOVITIATE; or, THE JESUIT IN TRAINING.

Being A YEAR AMONG THE ENGLISH JESUITS: a Personal Narrative. By ANDREW STEINMETZ. Second Edition, with Memoir and Portrait of the Author. In one vol. post 8vo. price 7s. 6d. bound in cloth.

"This is a remarkable book—a revealer of secrets, and full of materials for thought. .... It is written with every appearance of strict and honourable truthfulness. It describes, with a welcome minuteness, the daily, nightly, hourly occupations of the Jesuit Novitiates at Stonyhurst, their religious exercises and manners, in private and together; and depicts, with considerable acuteness and power, the conflicts of an intelligent, susceptible, honest-purposed spirit, while passing through such a process. If our readers should be disposed to possess themselves of this volume, it will be their own fault if the reading of it be profitless."—*British Quarterly Review*.

"This is as singular a book of its kind as has appeared since Blanco White's 'Letters of Doblado,' with the advantage of dealing with the Jesuits in England, instead of Popery in Spain. .... It will be found a very curious work."—*Spectator*.

"If it be desirable to know what is that mode of training by which the Jesuit system prepares its novices for their duties, this is the book to inform us, for it is a chronicle of actual experience. . . . The work of Mr Steinmetz is throughout marked by great fairness, . . . he neither conceals nor exaggerates; a spirit of candour pervades the whole narrative. . . . Could we know the experience of other novices, we should find that all have undergone, with more or less intensity, the process so vividly described in this volume. . . . It is written in an extremely animated style. The author's thoughts are original, and the passages relating to his personal history and feelings are agreeably introduced, and add to the interest of his narrative. It is a sufficient proof of his accuracy, that, though the Jesuits have many pens in this country, not one has been hardy enough to impugn a sentence of his statements."—*Britannia*.

"Mr. Steinmetz writes a most singular and interesting account of the Jesuit seminary, and his way of life there. . . . He seems to be a perfectly honest and credible informer, and his testimony may serve to enlighten many a young devotional aspirant who is meditating 'submission' to Rome, and the chain and scourge systems. There is nothing in the least resembling invective in the volume."—*Morning Chronicle*.

"At a time when Jesuitism seems to be rising once more, any work on this subject comes very opportunely. How the writer became a member of this mysterious body gives a key to the character of the man himself, and the spirit of his book. . . This narrative is well written, and as interesting as we expected."—*Weekly Chronicle*.

"The work has all the interest of a romance, and yet we do not believe that any portion of it is fictitious. . . . The author writes well, and evinces a strong and disciplined mind. The picture he draws of Jesuitism is a fearful one. The reader will find abundant matter for grave consideration in this most singular and striking volume."—*John Bull*.

"A more remarkable work it has seldom been our fortune to peruse. We hear and read much of the Quietism and Passive Obedience inculcated amongst the Jesuit body; but here we become personal spectators of these principles in action. . . . Mr. Steinmetz appears to be a most remarkable character. He may be received as an unbiassed witness. . . . We repeat it, Mr. Steinmetz's book is most valuable; earnest and truthful in its tone, and extremely interesting in its detail."—*New Quarterly Review*.

THE JESUIT IN THE FAMILY.

A Tale. By ANDREW STEINMETZ. In one vol. post 8vo. price 9s. cloth.

"A well-written and powerful novel, constructed for the development of Jesuit practices, and to show the Jesuit in action. The interest in some parts is intensely wrought up. Mr. Steinmetz has produced a work of no ordinary character, full of talent and full of interest."—*John Bull*.

"Remarkable for force of ideas and originality of style. * * * The narrative is dramatic, both in construction and language, and marked with great vivacity. In the conduct of the story and action of the personages, Mr. Steinmetz shows that he has closely studied human life, and profited by his observations. Indeed, we recollect no recent fiction that gives a more acute exposition of the varieties of individual character."—*Britannia*.

FIRST SERIES OF TALES OF THE COLONIES.
TALES OF THE COLONIES; OR, THE ADVENTURES OF AN EMIGRANT.

By CHARLES ROWCROFT, Esq., a late Colonial Magistrate. The Fifth Edition. In foolscap 8vo., price 6s. cloth.

"'Tales of the Colonies' is an able and interesting book. The author has the first great requisite in fiction—a knowledge of the life he undertakes to describe; and his matter is solid and real."—*Spectator*.

"This is a *book*, as distinguished from one of the bundles of waste paper in three divisions, calling themselves 'novels.'"—*Athenæum*.

"The narration has a deep and exciting interest. No mere romance, no mere fiction, however skilfully imagined or powerfully executed, can surpass it. The work to which it bears the nearest similitude is Robinson Crusoe, and it is scarcely, if at all inferior to that extraordinary history."—*John Bull*.

"Since the time of Robinson Crusoe, literature has produced nothing like these 'Tales of the Colonies.'"—*Metropolitan Magazine*.

".... Romantic literature does not supply instances of wonderful escape more marvellous. ... The book is manifestly a mixture of fact and fiction, yet it gives, we have every reason to believe, a true picture of a settler's life in that country; and is thickly interspersed with genuine and useful information."
Chambers's Edinburgh Journal.

"The contents of the first volume surpass in interest many of the novels of Sir Walter Scott."—*Westminster Review*.

"An exceedingly lively and interesting narrative, which affords a more striking view of the habits of emigrant colonial life than all the regular treatises, statistical returns, and even exploratory tours which we have read. ... It combines the fidelity of truth with the spirit of a romance, and has altogether so much of De Foe in its character and composition, that whilst we run we learn, and, led along by the variety of the incidents, become real ideal settlers in Van Diemen's Land."—*Literary Gazette*.

SECOND SERIES OF TALES OF THE COLONIES.
THE BUSHRANGER OF VAN DIEMEN'S LAND.

By C. ROWCROFT, Esq., Author of "Tales of the Colonies." In 3 vols. post 8vo. price 1l. 11s. 6d.

"These volumes have the same qualities that gained so much popularity for the Author's previous work 'Tales of the Colonies.' No one has depicted colonial life, as manifested in the settlements of Australia, with so much vigour and truth as Mr. Rowcroft. He rather seems to be a narrator of actual occurrences than an inventor of imaginary ones. His characters, his manners, and his scenes are all real. He has been compared to De Foe, and the comparison is just."—*Britannia*.

"These volumes form a second series of 'Tales of the Colonies,' and the pages are marked by the same vigorous and graphic pen which procured such celebrity for the first series. The interest, generally well sustained throughout, is occasionally of the most absorbing and thrilling kind. Altogether, there is a freshness about these volumes which brings them out in strong contrast to the vapid productions with which the press is teeming."—*Globe*.

"The story contains all the merits of the 'Tales of the Colonies' as regards style; being simple and *Crusoite*, if we might use the term, in its narrative. Mr. Rowcroft possesses invention to an extraordinary degree, in the manner in which he manages the escapes of the bushranger,—and he produces, by the simplest incidents, most interesting scenes;—pictures of nature and of a society totally different from anything to be found elsewhere."—*Weekly Chronicle*.

FANNY THE LITTLE MILLINER; OR, THE RICH AND THE POOR.

By CHARLES ROWCROFT, Esq. In one vol. 8vo., handsomely bound in cloth gilt, with Plates, price 14s.—The twelve parts may be had separately, price 1s. each, sewed.

AGRICULTURAL IMPROVEMENT.

THE FARMER'S FRIEND. A Periodical Record of Recent Discoveries, Improvements, and Practical Suggestions in Agriculture. One volume, post 8vo. price 7s. 6d. cloth.

"This may emphatically be called "The Farmer's Friend." It is one of the most valuable and complete farming books that has been published, and ought to be in the hands of every farmer."—*Sunderland Times.*

"Decidedly one of the most useful books: a really excellent work."—*Cumberland Pacquet.*

"A more valuable and important addition to the book shelf of the English yeoman can scarcely be made."—*Nottingham Mercury.*

"A most excellent work."—*Cambridge Advertiser.*

"We recommend this work to every farmer."—*Bridgewater Times.*

"This admirable work every practical farmer in the land should have in his possession."—*Cheltenham Journal.*

"A cheap and sterling work."—*Oxford Herald.*

"The best adjunct to the farmer."—*Kentish Observer.*

THE INDIAN MEAL BOOK:

Comprising the best American Receipts for the various Preparations of that excellent Article. By ELIZA LESLIE, of Philadelphia; Author of "American Domestic Cookery;" "The House Book;" "Seventy-five Receipts;" "French Cookery;" &c. &c. Second Edition. Foolscap 8vo. sewed in a wrapper, price 1s. 6d.

"Next to the corn itself, we cannot conceive a more acceptable present to the poor of any neighbourhood, either individually or in parochial libraries, than Miss Leslie's work. It is very simple, and embraces recipes for every purpose to which maize is put in the United States, and therefore cannot but add to the comfort of the too limited table of the labouring man."—*Indian News.*

"This little volume contains about sixty receipts for different preparations of Indian meal, and all of which may be found useful in the threatened dearth. Maize, or Indian corn, is now admitted to be the best and *most available* substitute for the potato."—*Economist.*

A FAMILIAR EXPLANATION OF THE ART OF ASSAYING GOLD AND SILVER;

And its bearing upon the Interests of the Public demonstrated; with considerations on the Importance of the Pix Jury; a Review of the past and present state of the Goldsmiths' Trade; and a Table, showing the mixture and sterling value per ounce of every quality of Gold that can be alloyed. By JAMES H. WATHERSTON, Goldsmith. 12mo., price 3s. 6d. cloth.

REV. H. MACKENZIE'S COMMENTARY.

COMMENTARY ON THE HOLY GOSPELS,

Arranged according to the TABLE OF LESSONS FOR DAILY SERVICE; designed for Family Reading. By the Rev. HENRY MACKENZIE, M.A., of Pembroke College, Oxford; Incumbent of Great Yarmouth. 8vo., price 7s. 6d. cloth; or in Five Parts, at 1s. 3d. each.

ON THE SITE OF THE HOLY SEPULCHRE.

With a Map of Jerusalem. By GEORGE FINLAY, Esq., K.R.G., Author of "Greece under the Romans." In 8vo., price 1s. 6d. sewed.

A NARRATIVE OF THE RECOVERY OF H. M. S. GORGON.

(CHARLES HOTHAM, Esq. Captain), Stranded in the Bay of Monte Video, May 10, 1844. By ASTLEY COOPER KEY, Commander, R.N. (late Lieut. of H. M. S. Gorgon.) 1 vol. 8vo. with numerous Plates. Price 7s. 6d. cloth.

MR. PRIDHAM'S ACCOUNT OF THE COLONIES.
ENGLAND'S COLONIAL EMPIRE.

An HISTORICAL, POLITICAL, and STATISTICAL ACCOUNT of the BRITISH EMPIRE, its COLONIES and DEPENDENCIES. By CHARLES PRIDHAM, Esq., B.A., Member of the Royal Geographical Society, &c.

VOLUME I.—Comprising

THE MAURITIUS AND ITS DEPENDENCIES.

"The first volume of a work intended to completely exhibit England's Colonial Empire. The author is Mr. Pridham, who, in a modest preface, apologises for having at so early an age undertaken so gigantic a task. The first volume, however, shows no lack of either ability, research, or knowledge. It is occupied with an excellent account of the Mauritius, divided into four parts: the first part gives its history from its discovery by the Portuguese to the present time; the second describes its inhabitants, and their institutions and states; the third its physical features and natural productions; and the fourth its industry, commerce, and government. Ample information is given on all these heads, and regarding the extent of the author's design, and the evidence he gives of the requisite qualification to carry it out satisfactorily, we make no doubt that his work will be a valuable addition to the history and geography of our colonial empire. The present volume is complete in itself."—*Britannia*.

"This is the first volume of what promises to be an important national work. The instalment now before us is brimful of valuable and interesting information, making up by far the most complete account of Mauritius which has yet been given to the world. The author has the qualifications necessary to the due fulfilment of the task which he has set himself. He is patient and pains-taking, accurate and impartial."—*Atlas*.

"This is the first volume of a series, which we hope to see completed in the spirit which the task has been undertaken. As a whole, we are bound to say, that the book is a standard one, and that 'England's Colonial Empire' has met with a chronicler of zeal, industry, and ability."—*Colonial Gazette*.

"There is no other such description of the Mauritius extant. The author has not only consulted the best, and perhaps all the authorities, but he has added information of his own, apparently gathered on the spot."—*Economist*.

THE COMMUNICATIONS BETWEEN EUROPE AND INDIA THROUGH EGYPT,

Considered in relation to the Political and Commercial Interests of Great Britain, and the Policy of France. By GEORGE FINLAY, Esq., K.R.G., Author of "Greece under the Romans."—In 8vo., price 2s. 6d.

"A well-written and very interesting pamphlet on a subject of immense interest to the government and people of Britain, and one on which, we are afraid, sufficient attention has not been bestowed by the authorities in this country."—*Cumberland Pacquet*.

CLINICAL ILLUSTRATIONS OF THE DISEASES OF INDIA:

As Exhibited in the MEDICAL HISTORY OF A BODY OF EUROPEAN SOLDIERS, for a Series of Years from their Arrival in that Country. By WILLIAM GEDDES, M.D., Member of the Royal Medical Society of Edinburgh, and the Medical and Physical Society of Calcutta, and late Surgeon of the Madras European Regiment. In one vol. 8vo. Price 16s. cloth.

"It is hardly possible to conceive a more complete medical history than the one furnished by Dr. Geddes. He has conferred an inestimable benefit upon medical science; and no practitioner who regards either his interest or his duty can be without the book."—*Indian News*.

"To the medical officers in India, and especially to those about to proceed thither, this will be found a valuable book of reference, and well merits to be included in the list of works with which officers are required to provide themselves on joining the service."—*British and Foreign Medical Review*.

"We strongly recommend every medical man going to the East Indies to have a copy of it at his side, as affording an excellent pattern for him to follow in the accumulation and arrangement of his observations when engaged in practice. Dr. Geddes has done for the symptoms of the diseases which he describes what Louis has done for the microscopic phenomena of fever."—*Medico-Chirurgical Review*.

"The leading characters of this volume are great precision and accuracy. This work must be referred to as a source of correct information on most questions relating to the diseases prevalent among Europeans in India."—*Edinburgh Medical and Surgical Journal*.

"The book will be valuable to every future practitioner as a means of knowing the success of certain methods of treating the diseases of India; and the student will find in it a minute description of those diseases which he is most likely to meet, should he be destined to serve in the East."—*Lancet*.

Scientific Works Illustrated.

COMPLETION OF
SIR JOHN HERSCHEL'S SURVEY OF THE HEAVENS.

RESULTS OF ASTRONOMICAL OBSERVATIONS,

Made during the years 1834, 5, 6, 7, 8, at the Cape of Good Hope; being the completion of a Telescopic Survey of the whole surface of the visible Heavens, commenced in 1825. By Sir JOHN HERSCHEL, Bart., K.H., M.A., D.C.L., F.R.S., L. & E., Hon. M.R.I.A., P.R.A.S., F.G.S., M.C.U.P.S., &c. &c. &c.

In 1 vol. royal 4to., with 18 Plates, price Four Guineas.

UNDER THE AUSPICES OF H. M. GOVERNMENT, AND OF THE HON. THE COURT OF DIRECTORS OF THE EAST INDIA COMPANY.

FAUNA ANTIQUA SIVALENSIS,

THE FOSSIL ZOOLOGY OF THE SEWALIK HILLS, in the North of India. By HUGH FALCONER, M.D., F.R.S., F.L.S., F.G.S., Member of the Asiatic Society of Bengal, and of the Royal Asiatic Society; of the Bengal Medical Service, and late Superintendent of the H. E. I. C. Botanic Garden at Saharunpoor: and PROBY T. CAUTLEY, F.G.S., Major in the Bengal Artillery, Member of the Asiatic Society of Bengal, &c. Edited by Dr. HUGH FALCONER. The Fossil Bones, drawn from nature and on stone, by G. H. FORD, and Assistants.

Plan of Publication.—The work will appear in about Twelve Parts, to be published at intervals of four months; each Part containing from Twelve to Fifteen folio Plates. The descriptive Letterpress will be printed in royal octavo. Price of each Part, one Guinea.— Part I. contains PROBOSCIDEA.—Parts II. and III., containing the continuation of PROBOSCIDEA, will be published shortly. Prospectuses of the Work may be obtained of the Publishers.

" A work of immense labour and research. . . . . Nothing has ever appeared in lithography in this country at all comparable to these plates; and as regards the representations of minute osseous texture, by Mr. Ford, they are perhaps the most perfect that have yet been produced in any country. . . . The work has commenced with the Elephant group, in which the authors say ' is most signally displayed the numerical richness of forms which characterises the Fossil Fauna of India;' and the first chapter relates to the Proboscidea—Elephant and Mastodon. The authors have not restricted themselves to a description of the Sewalik Fossil forms, but they propose to trace the affinities, and institute an arrangement of all the well-determined species in the family. They give a brief historical sketch of the leading opinions which have been entertained by palæontologists respecting the relations of the Mastodon and Elephant to each other, and of the successive steps in the discovery of new forms which have led to the modifications of these opinions. They state that the results to which they themselves have been conducted, lead them to differ on certain points from the opinions most commonly entertained at the present day, respecting the fossil species of Elephant and Mastodon."— *Address of the President of the Geological Society of London,* 20th Feb. 1846.

WORKS RECENTLY PUBLISHED AND IN PROGRESS UNDER THE AUTHORITY OF THE LORDS COMMISSIONERS OF THE ADMIRALTY.

₊ *In order to secure to science the full advantage of Discoveries in Natural History, the Lords Commissioners of Her Majesty's Treasury have been pleased to make a liberal grant of money towards defraying part of the expenses of the following important publications. They have, in consequence, been undertaken on a scale worthy of the high patronage thus received, and are offered to the public at a much lower price than would otherwise have been possible.*

I.

ILLUSTRATIONS OF THE ZOOLOGY OF SOUTH AFRICA.

Comprising all the new species of Quadrupeds, Birds, Reptiles, and Fishes, obtained during the Expedition fitted out by "The Cape of Good Hope Association for exploring Central Africa," in the years 1834, 1835, and 1836, with Letterpress Descriptions, and a Summary of African Zoology. By ANDREW SMITH, M.D., Surgeon to the Forces, and Director of the Expedition. In Royal Quarto Parts, price 10s. and 12s. each, containing on an average ten beautifully coloured Engravings, with descriptive Letterpress. Twenty-four Parts are now published.

II.

THE ZOOLOGY OF THE VOYAGE OF H.M.S. SULPHUR,

Under the Command of Captain Sir EDWARD BELCHER, R.N., C.B. F.R.G.S., &c. Edited and Superintended by RICHARD BRINSLEY HINDS, Esq., Surgeon R.N., attached to the Expedition.

Among the countries visited by the "Sulphur," and which in the present state of science are invested with more particular interest, may be mentioned the Californias, Columbia River, the North-west coast of America, the Feejee Group (a portion of the Friendly Islands), New Zealand, New Ireland, New Guinea, China, and Madagascar.

In Royal Quarto Parts, price 10s. each, with beautifully coloured Plates.

THIS WORK IS NOW COMPLETE, and may be had in sewed Parts, price 5l., or in half-russia, or cloth binding, at a small addition to the price.—Parts I. and II. contain MAMMALIA, by J. E. GRAY, Esq., F.R.S.—Parts III. and IV. BIRDS, by J. GOULD, Esq., F.L.S.—Parts V., IX., and X. FISH, by J. RICHARDSON, M.D., F.R.S.—Parts VI., VII., and VIII. SHELLS, by R. B. HINDS, Esq.

III.

THE BOTANY OF THE VOYAGE OF H.M.S. SULPHUR,

Under the Command of Captain Sir EDWARD BELCHER, R.N., C.B. F.R.G.S., &c., during the years 1836—42. Edited and Superintended by RICHARD BRINSLEY HINDS, Esq., Surgeon R.N., attached to the Expedition. The Botanical Descriptions by GEORGE BENTHAM, Esq.

THIS WORK IS NOW COMPLETE, and may be had in six sewed Parts, price 3l., or in half-russia, or cloth binding, at a small addition to the price.

PUBLISHED WITH THE APPROVAL OF THE LORDS COMMISSIONERS OF HER MAJESTY'S TREASURY.

GEOLOGICAL OBSERVATIONS MADE DURING THE VOYAGE OF H.M.S. BEAGLE,

Under the Command of CAPTAIN FITZROY, R.N.

Part I.—On Coral Formations.

By CHARLES DARWIN, M.A., F.R.S., Sec. G. S., &c. Demy 8vo., with Plates and Woodcuts, price 15s. in cloth.

Part II.—On the Volcanic Islands of the Atlantic and Pacific Oceans.

Together with a brief Notice of the Geology of the Cape of Good Hope, and of part of Australia. By CHARLES DARWIN, M.A., Esq. Price 10s. 6d. demy 8vo. cloth, with Map.

Part III.—On the Geology of South America.

By CHARLES DARWIN, M.A., Esq. Demy 8vo., with Map and Plates, price 12s. cloth.

AN INQUIRY INTO THE NATURE AND COURSE OF STORMS IN THE INDIAN OCEAN,

SOUTH OF THE EQUATOR; with a view of discovering their Origin, Extent, Rotatory Character, Rate and Direction of Progression, Barometrical Depression, and other concomitant phenomena; for the practical purpose of enabling ships to ascertain the proximity and relative position of Hurricanes; with suggestions on the means of avoiding them. By ALEXANDER THOM, Surgeon 86th Royal County Down Regiment. In one vol. 8vo., with Map and Plates, price 12s. cloth.

"The work before us is most valuable to seamen. . . . Mr. Thom gives us the result of his observations at the Mauritius; a station which is peculiarly well adapted for observing the hurricanes of the Indian Ocean, the ravages of which seamen have annually experienced; and those observations, combined with the results obtained by indefatigable enquiry, have entitled him to the gratitude of seamen, who may now profit by them. . . Mr. Thom's theory is rational and philosophical, and to us it is most satisfactory. . . . There are important considerations for seamen in this work."—*Nautical Magazine.*

"The author proceeds in strict accordance with the principles of inductive philosophy, and collects all his facts before he draws his inferences or propounds a theory. His statements are so full and clear, and drawn from such simple sources, yet are so decisive in their tendency, that we think there can be no doubt he has established the rotatory action of storms. The practical application of his investigations are too palpable to be missed."—*Britannia.*

A DISSERTATION ON THE TRUE AGE OF THE EARTH,

AS ASCERTAINED FROM THE HOLY SCRIPTURES. Containing a Review of the Opinions of Ancient and Modern Chronologers, including Usher, Hales, Clinton, and Cuninghame; and a Chronological Table of the Principal Epochs and Events in Sacred and Profane History, from the Creation to the Present Time. By PROFESSOR WALLACE. In demy 8vo., price 12s. cloth.

"It is learned and laborious."—*Britannia.*

EXPERIMENTAL RESEARCHES, CHEMICAL AND AGRICULTURAL.

Part I. contains—Carbon a Compound Body made by Plants, in quantities varying with the circumstances under which they are placed.—Part II. Decomposition of Carbon during the Putrefactive Fermentation. By ROBERT RIGG, F.R.S. In demy 8vo., price 7s. 6d.

ILLUSTRATED WORKS ON NATURAL HISTORY BY CAPTAIN THOMAS BROWN.

ILLUSTRATIONS OF THE RECENT CONCHOLOGY OF GREAT BRITAIN AND IRELAND.

With the Description and Localities of all the Species,—Marine, Land, and Fresh-Water. Drawn and Coloured from Nature, by Captain THOMAS BROWN, F.L.S., M.W.S., M.K.S., Member of the Manchester Geological Society. In one vol. royal 4to., illustrated with fifty-nine beautifully coloured Plates, price 63s. cloth.

ILLUSTRATIONS OF THE FOSSIL CONCHOLOGY OF GREAT BRITAIN AND IRELAND.

By Captain THOMAS BROWN, F.L.S. To be completed in about Thirty Numbers, each containing four Plates. Royal 4to., price 3s. coloured, and 2s. plain.

Twenty-eight Numbers have appeared, and the work will soon be completed.

ILLUSTRATIONS OF THE GENERA OF BIRDS.

Embracing their Generic Characters, with Sketches of their Habits, By Captain THOMAS BROWN, F.L.S. Now publishing in Numbers, royal 4to., each containing four Plates, price 3s. coloured.

Part I. is just completed, price 36s. cloth.

THE ELEMENTS OF FOSSIL CONCHOLOGY;

According to the Arrangement of Lamarck; with the newly-established Genera of other Authors. By Captain THOMAS BROWN, F.L.S. With twelve Plates, fcap. 8vo., price 5s. cloth.

ALPHABETICAL LIST OF THE SHELLS OF GREAT BRITAIN AND IRELAND;

Embracing the Nomenclature of LAMARCK, GRAY, TURTON, and BROWN, for the purpose of effecting exchanges and naming collections. On a sheet, price 1s.

Miscellaneous.

THE DUTIES OF JUDGE ADVOCATES,

Compiled from HER MAJESTY'S and the HON. EAST INDIA COMPANY'S MILITARY REGULATIONS, and from the Works of various Writers on Military Law. By Captain R. M. HUGHES, 12th Regiment Bombay Army; Deputy Judge-Advocate General, Scinde Field Force. In one vol. post 8vo., price 7s. cloth.

"Captain Hughes's little volume on this important subject will well supply the absence of that full and particular information which officers suddenly appointed to act as 'Deputy Judge Advocates' must have felt the want of, even though tolerably well versed in military law."—*Spectator*.

"A professional *vade-mecum*, relating to most important duties, and executed in the ablest manner. We consider this, the only complete separate treatise on the subject, to be one of great value, and deserving the study of every British officer."—*Lit. Gazette*.

"This book is a digest as well as a compilation, and may be emphatically called 'The Hand-Book of Military Justice.'"—*Atlas*.

"We recommend the work to every British officer."—*Army and Navy Register*.

THE NOTE-BOOK OF A NATURALIST.

By E. P. THOMPSON. Post 8vo., price 9s. cloth.

"The author of this modestly-styled 'Note-Book' not only possesses and communicates scientific intelligence, but he has travelled far and near, and from very infancy been devoted to natural history. . . . . We rely on the quotations to support our opinion of the very agreeable and various character of this volume."—*Literary Gazette*.

"In all that relates to original observation the 'Note-Book of a Naturalist' is agreeable, interesting, and fresh. . . . The more original and numerous passages may vie with the observations of Jesse. In fact, there is a considerable resemblance between the two authors. Anecdote is substantially the character of the better part."—*Spectator*.

LIFE IN NORTH WALES.

LLEWELLYN'S HEIR;

Or, NORTH WALES; its MANNERS, CUSTOMS, and SUPERSTITIONS during the last Century, illustrated by a Story founded on Facts. In three vols. post 8vo., price 1l. 11s. 6d.

"It is a real work, with more material and original knowledge than half the manufactured novels that appear in these days."—*Spectator*.

"We can most cordially recommend it as a series of Sketches of North Wales well worthy of perusal; so various and so curious as to be as welcome to the library of the antiquary and portfolio of the artist as to the leisure hour of the novel reader."—*Literary Gazette*.

A NEW SPIRIT OF THE AGE.

Containing Critical Essays, and Biographical Sketches of Literary and other Eminent Characters of the Present Time. Edited by R. H. HORNE, Esq., Author of "Orion," "Gregory the Seventh," &c. &c. These volumes are illustrated with Engravings on steel, from new and original Portraits of DICKENS, TENNYSON, CARLYLE, WORDSWORTH, TALFOURD, BROWNING, SOUTHWOOD SMITH, and Miss MARTINEAU. Second Edition, Revised by the Editor, with "Introductory Comments." In 2 vols. post 8vo., price 24s. cloth.

"Two volumes of clever and subtile dissertation on the merits of almost every living writer of any pretension, written in a very animated and pleasant style."—*Morning Herald*, March 25, 1844.

"Mr. Horne's admirations appear to us to be well placed, and his sympathies generous and noble."—*Morning Chronicle*.

CHRISTMAS FESTIVITIES: TALES, SKETCHES, AND CHARACTERS.

With BEAUTIES OF THE MODERN DRAMA, in Four Specimens. By JOHN POOLE, Esq., Author of "Paul Pry," &c. &c. In one vol. post 8vo., price 10s. 6d. cloth, with a Portrait of the Author.

"A capital book for the season."—*Britannia*.

PRYINGS OF A POSTMAN.

In one vol. post 8vo., price 5s.

OUR ACTRESSES;

Or, GLANCES AT STAGE FAVOURITES, PAST and PRESENT. By Mrs. C. BARON WILSON, Authoress of the "Life of the Duchess of St. Albans," "Memoirs of Monk Lewis," &c. &c. In 2 vols. post 8vo., illustrated with numerous Engravings on Steel, from new and original Portraits, price 24s. cloth.

"Handsome volumes, adorned with several portraits, and the biographies are full of amusing anecdotes."—*Atlas*.

"So attractive are the stage and its denizens that considerable amusement will be derived from the perusal of these pages."—*Literary Gazette*.

THE HOME BOOK; OR, YOUNG HOUSEKEEPER'S ASSISTANT.

Forming a Complete System of DOMESTIC ECONOMY, and Household Accounts. With Estimates of Expenditure, &c. &c., in every Department of Housekeeping. Founded on Forty-five years personal experience. By a LADY. 12mo., price 5s., boards.

THE HOME ACCOUNT-BOOK; OR, HOUSEKEEPER'S REGISTER OF FAMILY EXPENSES.

Arranged upon the improved system recommended in the "Home Book;" and exhibiting the Weekly, Monthly, Quarterly, and Annual Expenditure for every article of Domestic consumption. For the use of either large or small Families. By the Author of the "THE HOME BOOK." Post 4to., half-bound, price 4s. 6d.

"These two useful little volumes form the most complete system of Domestic Management for the guidance of the young Housekeeper that has ever appeared. Of the Home Book we cannot speak too highly."—*Gentleman's Magazine*.

"Incomparably the best arranged work of its class that we have seen."—*La Belle Assemblée*.

A COMPREHENSIVE HISTORY OF THE WOOLLEN TRADE.

From the earliest Records to the present Period, comprising the Woollen and Worsted Manufactures, and the Natural and Commercial History of Sheep, with the various Breeds and Modes of Management in different Countries. By JAMES BISCHOFF, Esq. In two large volumes, 8vo., illustrated with Plates, price 1l. 6s. cloth.

"Mr. Bischoff's work will be found valuable to all persons interested in the subject."—*Athenæum*.

"Mr. Bischoff has in these volumes collected a vast mass of curious and valuable information, acceptable to readers of varied tastes, even though quite unconnected with manufactures and trade. We recommend every reader to peruse attentively this meritorious compilation.—We finally recommend these volumes of Mr. Bischoff's to the careful consideration of all those interested in the subjects of which they treat."—*Times*.

A COMPREHENSIVE HISTORY OF THE IRON TRADE

THROUGHOUT THE WORLD, from the earliest Records to the present Time. With an Appendix, containing Official Tables, and other public Documents. By HARRY SCRIVENOR, Esq., Blaenavon. In one vol. demy 8vo., price 15s. cloth.

"Mr. Scrivenor's History is written with elaborate research and anxious care, and goes into and exhausts the entire subject; it contains numerous facts full of interest to common readers."—*Tait's Magazine.*

THE BRITISH MERCHANT'S ASSISTANT.

Containing:—Part I. Tables of Simple Interest at 3, 3½, 4, 4½, and 5 per cent.—Part II. Tables showing the Interest on Exchequer Bills at 1½d., 1¾d., 2d., 2¼d., 2½d., 3d., 3¼d., and 3½d. per cent. per diem.—Part III. Tables for Ascertaining the Value of every description of English and Foreign Stock. Also the amount of Brokerage, Commission, Freight. Marine, and other Insurance, at every rate per cent., &c. &c. &c. By G. GREEN. Royal 8vo, price 1l. 11s. 6d. cloth. Each of the above Three Parts is sold separately.

ASSURANCES UPON LIVES,

A Familiar Explanation of the NATURE, ADVANTAGES, and IMPORTANCE arising therefrom, and the various Purposes to which they may be usefully applied: including also a particular Account of the routine required for Effecting a Policy; and of the different systems of Life Assurance now in use, the Principles, Terms, and Tables of Seventy London Assurance Offices, &c. By LEWIS POCOCK, F.S.A. In post 8vo, price 7s. cloth.

"There are no technicalities in Mr. Pocock's work to prevent its being useful to all; and those, therefore, who are likely to have recourse to Life Insurance will do wisely in consulting this familiar explanation of its nature and advantages."—*Globe.*

AN INQUIRY INTO THE CAUSES AND MODES OF THE WEALTH OF INDIVIDUALS;

Or, THE PRINCIPLES OF TRADE AND SPECULATION EXPLAINED. By THOMAS CORBET, Esq. Post 8vo, price 6s. cloth.

"Mr. Corbet deserves our best thanks for laying down so clearly and methodically his ideas on the subject of such vast importance."—*New Monthly Magazine.*

OUTLINES OF NAVAL ROUTINE;

Being a Concise and Complete Manual in Fitting, Refitting, Quartering, Stationing, Making and Shortening Sail, Heaving down, Rigging Shears, and, in short, performing all the ordinary duties of a Man-of-War, according to the best practice. By Lieutenant ALEXANDER D. FORDYCE, R.N. In royal 8vo, price 10s. 6d. boards.

SCENES IN THE LIFE OF A SOLDIER OF FORTUNE.

By a MEMBER OF THE IMPERIAL GUARDS. In 12mo., price 5s.

"This tale has a strange *personal* history. It purports to be the autobiography o an Italian soldier, who fought under the banners of the French Republic; and who, later in life, when become a teacher, told his story to an English traveller, his pupil, who has here set it down."—*Tait's Magazine.*

ESSAY ON THE LIFE AND INSTITUTIONS OF OFFA, KING OF MERCIA,

A.D. 755—794. By the Rev. HENRY MACKENZIE, M.A. In 8vo. price 3s. 6d. in cloth, gilt leaves.

"A very scholarly composition, displaying much research and information respecting the Anglo-Saxon institutions."—*Spectator.*

THE OBLIGATIONS OF LITERATURE TO THE MOTHERS OF ENGLAND.

PRIZE ESSAY, 1840. By CAROLINE A. HALSTED. In one vol. post 8vo., price 5s. neatly bound in cloth.

"The object of the writer has been to show the services rendered by the mothers of England to religion and the state, and to science and learning generally; and the examples adduced display considerable knowledge and research, and are always happily selected and placed in the most attractive point of view."—*Britannia*.

THE LIFE OF MARGARET BEAUFORT,

COUNTESS OF RICHMOND AND DERBY, and Mother of King Henry the Seventh, Foundress of Christ's and of St. John's College, Oxford; Being the Historical Memoir for which the Honorary Premium was awarded by the Directors of the Gresham Commemoration, Crosby Hall. By CAROLINE A. HALSTED, Author of "Investigation," &c. In one vol. demy 8vo., with a Portrait, price 12s.

"This work cannot fail of success. The subject is deeply interesting, and has been hitherto almost unexplored. The style is chaste and correct, and it has high claims to popularity wide and permanent. On many topics the authoress has accumulated some valuable historical details from sources which have not hitherto been consulted, and has thus compiled a work which, if not entitled to rank amongst the 'curiosities of literature,' s at least one of the most interesting and instructive books of the season."—*Atlas*.

THE LAST OF THE PLANTAGENETS:

An Historical Narrative, illustrating some of the Public Events and Domestic and Ecclesiastical Manners of the Fifteenth and Sixteenth Centuries. Third Edition. In one vol. fcap. 8vo., price 7s. 6d. cloth boards.

"This is a work that must make its way into a permanent place in our literature. The quaintness of its language, the touching simplicity of its descriptions and dialogues, and the reverential spirit of love which breathes through it, will insure it a welcome reception amongst all readers of refined taste and discernment."—*Atlas*.

ANGLO-SAXON LITERATURE.

ANALECTA ANGLO-SAXONICA.

A SELECTION, in PROSE and VERSE from ANGLO-SAXON AUTHORS of various Ages; with a GLOSSARY. By BENJAMIN THORPE, F.S.A. A New Edition, corrected and revised. Post 8vo., price 12s. cloth.

THE ANGLO-SAXON VERSION OF THE STORY OF APOLLONIUS OF TYRE,

Upon which is founded the Play of "PERICLES," attributed to Shakspeare; from a MS. in the Library of Christ Church College, Cambridge. With a Literal Translation, &c. By BENJAMIN THORPE, F.S.A. Post 8vo., price 6s.

A GRAMMAR OF THE ANGLO-SAXON TONGUE,

With a PRAXIS. By ERASMUS RASK, Professor of Literary History in, and Librarian to, the University of Copenhagen, &c. &c. A New Edition, enlarged and improved by the Author. Translated from the Danish, by B. THORPE, Honorary Member of the Icelandic Literary Society of Copenhagen. 8vo., price 12s.

Oriental and Colonial.

WAR WITH THE SIKHS.

THE PUNJAUB:

Being a brief account of the Country of the Sikhs, its Extent, History, Commerce, Productions, Government, Manufactures, Laws, Religion, &c. By LIEUT.-COL. STEINBACH, late of the Lahore Service. A new edition, revised, with additions, including an account of the recent events in the Punjaub. In post 8vo. price 5s. cloth, with Map. The Map may be had separately, price 1s. coloured, and 1s. 6d. in case.

"There is much information in this volume, condensed into brief space, about a people to whom late occurrences have given a common interest."—*Examiner*.

A VISIT TO THE ANTIPODES,

With some REMINISCENCES OF A SOJOURN IN AUSTRALIA. By A SQUATTER. In one vol. fcap. 8vo., with Illustrations, price 5s. cloth.

COMMENTARY ON THE HINDU SYSTEM OF MEDICINE.

By T. A. WISE, M.D., Member of the Royal College of Surgeons, and of the Royal Medical and Chirurgical Society, Corresponding Member of the Zoological Society of London, and of the Philomathic Society of Paris; Bengal Medical Service. In one vol. 8vo., price 12s. cloth.

NEW ZEALAND AND ITS ABORIGINES:

Being an Account of the Aborigines, Trade, and Resources of the Colony; and the advantages it now presents as a field for Emigration and the investment of Capital. By WILLIAM BROWN, lately a member of the Legislative Council of New Zealand. Post 8vo., price 8s. cloth.

"A very intelligent and useful book."—*Times*.

AN ACCOUNT OF THE SETTLEMENTS OF THE NEW ZEALAND COMPANY,

From Personal Observations during a residence there. By the Hon. HENRY WILLIAM PETRE. In demy 8vo., with a Map and Plates. Fifth Edition. Price 3s. cloth.

"This is a valuable contribution to our sources of information respecting New Zealand, and the best proof of the Author's very favourable opinion of the country, is his making immediate arrangements to return there as a Colonist."

SYDNEY AND MELBOURNE;

With Remarks on the Present State and Future Prospects of New South Wales, and Practical Advice to Emigrants of various classes; to which is added a Summary of the Route home, by India, Egypt, &c. By CHARLES JOHN BAKER, Esq. Post 8vo., price 8s. cloth.

TRAVELS IN NEW SOUTH WALES.

By ALEXANDER MARJORIBANKS. 1 vol. 12mo., price 7s. 6d. cloth.

NEW ZEALAND, SOUTH AUSTRALIA, AND NEW SOUTH WALES.

A Record of recent Travels in these Colonies, with especial reference to Emigration, and the advantageous employment of Labour and Capital. By R. G. JAMESON, Esq. Post 8vo., price 8s. cloth, with Maps and Plates.

"Mr. Jameson is an intelligent and unprejudiced observer, and has made good use of his faculties."—*Spectator*.

A SKETCH OF NEW SOUTH WALES.

By J. O. BALFOUR, Esq., for Six Years a Settler in the Bathurst District. Post 8vo., price 6s. cloth.

"To Emigrants to the quarter of which it treats it must be a valuable guide."
Literary Gazette.

CALIFORNIA: A HISTORY OF UPPER AND LOWER CALIFORNIA,

From their first discovery to the present Time; comprising an Account of the Climate, Soil, Natural Productions, Agriculture, Commerce, &c. A full view of the Missionary Establishments, and condition of the Free and domesticated Indians. With an Appendix, relating to Steam Navigation in the Pacific. Illustrated with a new Map, Plans of the Harbours, and numerous Engravings. By ALEXANDER FORBES, Esq. 8vo., price 14s. cloth.

SUGGESTIONS FOR A GENERAL PLAN OF RAPID COMMUNICATION BY STEAM NAVIGATION AND RAILWAYS,

And applying it to the Shortening the Time of Communication between the Eastern and Western Hemispheres. By EDWARD MCGEACHY, Esq., Crown Surveyor, Jamaica. With 2 maps, 8vo. price 3s. bds.

CHINA OPENED;

Or, a Display of the Topography, History, Customs, Manners, Arts, Manufactures, Commerce, Literature, Religion, Jurisprudence, &c., of the CHINESE EMPIRE. By the Rev. CHARLES GUTZLAFF. Revised by the Rev. ANDREW REED, D.D. In 2 vols., post 8vo., price 24s. cloth.

"We obtain from these volumes more information of a practical kind than from any other publication; a closer view of the Domestic life of the Chinese — of the public institutions—the manufactures—natural resources—and literature. The work in fact is full of information, gathered with diligence, and fairly leaves the English reader without any excuse for ignorance on the subject."—*Atlas*.

"This is by far the most interesting, complete, and valuable account of the Chinese Empire that has yet been published."—*Sun*.

A HISTORY OF THE CHINESE EMPIRE, ANCIENT AND MODERN.

Comprising a Retrospect of the Foreign Intercourse and Trade with China. Illustrated by a new and Corrected Map of the Empire. By the Rev. CHARLES GUTZLAFF. In 2 vols. demy 8vo. bds., price 28s.

"We cordially recommend this exceedingly interesting account of this very interesting country."—*London Review*.

"Mr. Gutzlaff has evidently combined industry with talent in producing this work, which far exceeds in information, research, and apparent veracity, anything we have before seen concerning this curious and singular nation."—*London News*.

HAND-BOOK FOR INDIA AND EGYPT:

Comprising Travels from Calcutta, through India, to the Himalaya Mountains, and a Voyage down the Sutlege and Indus Rivers; a Visit to the city of Hyderabad, in Scinde; and a Journey to England by the Red Sea and Mediterranean: with Descriptions of the Three Presidencies of India; and the fullest details for parties proceeding to any part of India, either by the Overland Route, or by way of the Cape of Good Hope. By GEORGE PARBURY, Esq., M.R.A.S. Second Edition, one vol. post 8vo., with an entirely new Map, price 12s. cloth.

⁎ The press, both of Great Britain and India, have combined in eulogizing the value of this work, but it may only here be needful to quote the following remarks from the editorial columns of the *Standard* of the 10th of April, 1843:—"We have elsewhere copied from Mr. Parbury's Hand-Book to India and Egypt, an interesting account of the City of Hyderabad. Let us, in acknowledgment of the means afforded to us to inform and gratify our readers, say of Mr. Parbury's work, as we may with truth, that it is the best Topographical Guide to the countries to which it refers we have ever seen, a most interesting book, independently of its topographical utility, and an almost indispensable key to the late transactions in Central Asia."

THE MODERN HISTORY AND CONDITION OF EGYPT.

Its CLIMATE, DISEASES, and CAPABILITIES; exhibited in a Personal Narrative of Travels in that Country, with an Account of the Proceedings of Mahommed Ali Pascha, from 1801 to 1843, interspersed with Illustrations of Scripture History, the Fulfilment of Prophecy, and the Progress of Civilization in the East. By W. HOLT YATES, M.D., &c. In two thick volumes, demy 8vo., with numerous Illustrations, price 34s. cloth.

"He fulfils his historic vocation by an ample resumé of the more prominent incidents which have distinguished the fortunes of the Pascha, upon whose policy of general monopoly his strictures are severe enough, and acquits himself creditably from his spirited and highly coloured sketches of the abundant objects to which he draws attention."—*Morning Herald*.

THE INVALID'S GUIDE TO MADEIRA.

With a Description of Teneriffe, Lisbon, Cintra, and Mafra; and a Vocabulary of the Portuguese and English Languages. By WILLIAM WHITE COOPER, M.R.C.S., Surgeon to the Hon. Artillery Company. In one vol. fcap. 8vo., price 4s. cloth gilt.

"There has recently been published a small work by Mr. Cooper, which may be consulted with advantage."—SIR JAMES CLARK *on Climate*.

NOTES AND OBSERVATIONS ON THE IONIAN ISLANDS AND MALTA;

With some REMARKS on CONSTANTINOPLE and TURKEY; and on the system of Quarantine, as at present conducted. By JOHN DAVY, M.D., F.R.SS., L. & E., Inspector-General of Army Hospitals, L.R. In two vols. demy 8vo., price 32s. cloth, with a large Map by Arrowsmith, and illustrated with Plates.

"Dr. Davy's work deserves to be bought as well as perused, so carefully, completely, and expensively has it been got up. We hope that the consciousness of having discharged such an important duty will not only be the result of his long labour, but that the work will prove as remunerative as it ought to be."—*Westminster Review*.

"There probably is not another work in our language in which so ample and substantially useful an account is given of the Ionian Islands as is here to be found. There can be little doubt that to these volumes will be assigned an honourable place amongst the recognised master-works of the class to which they belong."—*Morning Herald*.

THE NATURE AND PROPERTIES OF THE SUGAR CANE;

With Practical Directions for the Improvement of its Culture, and the Manufacture of its Products. To which is added an additional Chapter on the MANUFACTURE OF SUGAR FROM BEET-ROOT. By GEORGE RICHARDSON PORTER, F.R.S., Corresponding Member of the Institute of France. New Edition, demy 8vo., price 12s. cloth, revised throughout, with many additions and corrections by the Author, and illustrated with Plates.

THE ANGLO-INDIAN AND COLONIAL ALMANACK.

And CIVIL, MILITARY, and COMMERCIAL DIRECTORY for 1847. In post 8vo., price 2s. 6d. in ornamental wrapper.

The HOME DEPARTMENT of the Almanack comprises—I. CIVIL and ECCLESIASTICAL; including the Government offices and the India House; together with the forms of procedure, and educational studies, requisite for obtaining Civil Appointments, and all matters connected with those appointments, from the commencing salary to the retiring allowance.—II. MILITARY and MARINE; including information of a similar kind respecting these services, and the Home Establishment of the East India Company.—III. COMMERCIAL; containing Lists of Merchants, Agents, Associations, &c., throughout the United Kingdom; likewise, the trades connected with India and the Colonies; and Tariff of Indian and Colonial produce.

The EAST INDIAN AND COLONIAL DEPARTMENT embraces — I. CIVIL. The Government Lists of Bengal, Madras, Bombay, Ceylon, Hong Kong, Australia, New Zealand, Mauritius, and the Cape of Good Hope; Lists of Civil Servants and their appointments, and of Judicial Establishments, with a detailed account of the Benefit Funds.—II. MILITARY. Staff and Field Officers; Distribution of the Army, including the Royal troops; Ecclesiastical Establishment; and all Benefit Funds.—III. COMMERCIAL. List of Mercantile Firms, Banks, Insurance Companies, Public Institutions, &c., in India and the Colonies; with the respective Tariffs, and Tables of Money, Weights, Measures, &c., and other miscellaneous information.

Religious and Educational.

MRS. ELLIS'S MORAL FICTIONS.

PICTURES OF PRIVATE LIFE.

By Mrs. ELLIS, Author of the "Women of England," &c. &c. &c. Each Volume is complete in itself, and may be purchased separately. In 3 vols. fcap. 8vo. beautifully illustrated, price 7s. 6d. each, in a handsome and uniform cloth binding, or 10s. 6d. morocco. Contents:—

Vol. I. "OBSERVATIONS ON FICTITIOUS NARRATIVE," "THE HALL AND THE COTTAGE," "ELLEN ESKDALE," "THE CURATE'S WIDOW," and "MARRIAGE AS IT MAY BE."

Vol. II. "MISANTHROPY," and "THE PAINS OF PLEASING."

Vol. III. "PRETENSION; or, the FALLACIES OF FEMALE EDUCATION."

"I could give abundant evidence, gratuitously offered to the writer, that these simple stories were not sent forth to the world without some degree of adaptation to its wants and its condition."—*Author's Introduction.*

THE LIGHT OF MENTAL SCIENCE;

Being an ESSAY on MORAL TRAINING. By Mrs. LOUDON, Authoress of "First Love," "Dilemmas of Pride," &c. &c. In one vol. fcap. 8vo., price 3s. cloth.

"One of the most philosophical books we have seen for a long time."—*Observer.*

THE PARENT'S CABINET OF AMUSEMENT AND INSTRUCTION.

A valuable and instructive Present for the Young. Each volume of this useful and instructive little work comprises a variety of information on different subjects:—Natural History, Biography, Travels, &c.; Tales, original and selected; and animated Conversations on the objects that daily surround young people. The various tales and subjects are illustrated with Woodcuts. Each volume is complete in itself, and may be purchased separately. In six neatly bound vols., price 3s. 6d. each.

"Every parent at all interested in his children must have felt the difficulty of providing suitable reading for them in their hours of amusement. This little work presents these advantages in a considerable degree, as it contains just that description of reading which will be beneficial to young children."—*Quarterly Journal of Education.*

LITTLE STORIES FROM THE PARLOUR PRINTING-PRESS.

By the Author of "THE PARENT'S CABINET." Royal 18mo., price 2s. 6d. neatly bound in cloth.

"A very nice little book for children. The author has evidently been familiar with children, and brought himself to understand their feelings. No child's book that we have ever seen has been so admirably levelled at their capacities as this admirably written little book."—*Weekly Chronicle.*

THE JUVENILE MISCELLANY OF AMUSEMENT AND INSTRUCTION.

Illustrated by numerous Plates and Woodcuts. Fcap. 8vo., price 4s. 6d. neatly bound in cloth.

"Filled with amusement and instruction as its title indicates."—*Court Journal.*

INVESTIGATION; OR, TRAVELS IN THE BOUDOIR.

By CAROLINE A. HALSTED, Author of "The Life of Margaret Beaufort," &c. &c. Fcap. 8vo., with highly-finished Plates, 4s. 6d. cloth.

"This is an elegantly-written and highly instructive work for young people, in which a general knowledge of various interesting topics, connected with every-day life, is presented to the youthful mind in an attractive and amusing form."

THE PROGRESS OF CREATION,

Considered with reference to the PRESENT CONDITION OF THE EARTH. An interesting and useful work for young people. By MARY ROBERTS, Author of "Annals of My Village," &c. &c. In fcap. 8vo., beautifully illustrated, price 4s. 6d. cloth.

"We have seldom met with a work, in which instruction and entertainment are more happily blended."—*Times.*

"This beautiful volume forms an instructive collection of striking facts, interspersed with amiable reflections."—*Spectator.*

THE CHRISTIAN'S SUNDAY COMPANION.

Being Reflections, in Prose and Verse, on the Collect, Epistle, and Gospel; and Proper Lessons for each Sunday; with a view to the immediate connexion. By Mrs. J. A. SARGANT. In one vol. post 8vo., price 8s. cloth.

"We cordially recommend this volume as an acceptable present to be made to the heads of families, and also an admirable school book to be read on Sunday morning to scholars before proceeding to the Temple of God."—*Church and State Gazette.*

"The whole production is eminently fitted to elevate the tone of religious feeling, to strengthen in the minds not only of the rising generation, but also of the older friends to our venerable ecclesiastical institution, sentiments of firm and fervent attachment to the pure faith and reformed worship established in this Protestant country, and for these reasons especially we recommend it to the perusal of our readers."—*Norfolk Chronicle.*

THE RELIGIOUS HISTORY OF MAN;

In which RELIGION and SUPERSTITION are traced from their source. By D. MORISON. The Second Edition, enlarged, fcap. 8vo. price 6s. cloth.

"The intention of this book is not less admirable than the manner in which it is written. It is most instructive, and the tone of its contents is in the highest degree pious, without the least tinge of puritanism. The information it gives on the most difficult points of biblical reading renders it a valuable book to all who desire true knowledge."—*Age.*

"Curious, industrious, and learned, and well worthy the attention of the public."—*Literary Gazette.*

"The plan of this book was both extensive and important—embracing an inquiry into the nature of Revelation, and its influence on the opinions and customs of mankind;" * * * "the writer uses *Scripture* as an interpreter," and "sticks to the literal text of the six days."—*Spectator.*

THE FAMILY SANCTUARY;

A Form of Domestic Devotion for every Sabbath in the Year: containing the Collect of the Day; a Portion of Scripture; an Original Prayer or Sermon; and the Benediction. Second Edition. One vol. 8vo., price 7s. 6d. half bound in cloth.

WORKS BY THE REV. CHARLES B. TAYLER, M.A.

Author of "May you Like it," &c. &c.

"These are truly Christian Parents' Books, and happy would it be for the rising generation if their instructors and tutors would put these admirable works of Mr. Tayler into the hands of the young, while their tender minds are yet open to receive the good impressions which they are also calculated to convey."—*Christian Monitor.*

I.
RECORDS OF A GOOD MAN'S LIFE.

Seventh Edition, in one vol. small 8vo., price 7s. neatly bound in cloth.

II.
MONTAGUE; OR, IS THIS RELIGION?

A Page from the Book of the World. New Edition, in fcap. 8vo., Illustrated, price 6s. cloth, and 9s. morocco extra.

III.
A VOLUME OF SERMONS

On the Doctrines and Duties of Christianity. Second Edition, demy 12mo., price 5s. boards.

IV.
LEGENDS AND RECORDS, CHIEFLY HISTORICAL.

Contents:—Lucy—Lorenzo; or, a Vision of Conscience—The Lady Lisle—Fulgentius and Meta—Anne of Cleves; or, Katharine Howard—George the Third—The Lady Russell—Guyon of Marseilles—The Earl of Strafford—Donna Francesca—Joan of Kent—The Lady Anne Carr—The Son and Heir—Leonora. In post 8vo., beautifully Illustrated, price 10s. 6d. elegantly bound.

V.
THE CHILD OF THE CHURCH OF ENGLAND.

Price 2s. neatly half bound.

VI.
SOCIAL EVILS AND THEIR REMEDY.

A Series of Narratives. The First Number, entitled "The Mechanic," was pronounced to be "One of the most useful and interesting publications that had issued from the press."

The following are the Contents of the different Numbers, price 1s. 6d. each:—II. "The Lady and the Lady's Maid."—III. "The Pastor of Dronfells."—IV. "The Labourer and his Wife."—V. "The Country Town."—VI. "Live and Let Live; or, the Manchester Weavers."—VII. "The Soldier."—VIII. "The Leaside Farm." Every two consecutive Numbers form a Volume, which may be procured, neatly bound, price 4s. each.

"The design of Mr. Tayler is praiseworthy; his object being to counteract, by a series of tales illustrative of the power and necessity of religion in the daily and hourly concerns of life, 'the confusion of error with truth in Miss Martineau's Entertainig Stories.'"—*Christian Remembrancer.*

THE RECTORY OF VALEHEAD;

Or, THE EDIFICE OF A HOLY HOME. By the Rev. ROBERT WILSON EVANS, B.D., Vicar of Heversham. Thirteenth Edition, with an illustrative Plate, price 6s. neatly bound in cloth; or 9s. elegantly bound in morocco.

"Universally and cordially do we recommend this delightful volume. We believe no person could read this work and not be the better for its pious and touching lessons. It is a page taken from the book of life, and eloquent with all the instruction of an excellent pattern: it is a commentary on the affectionate warning, 'Remember thy Creator in the days of thy youth.' We have not for some time seen a work we could so deservedly praise, or so conscientiously recommend."—*Literary Gazette.*

THE LIFE-BOOK OF A LABOURER.

PRACTICAL LESSONS FOR INSTRUCTION AND GUIDANCE. By A WORKING CLERGYMAN, Author of the "Bishop's Daughter," &c. &c. In one vol. 8vo., price 7s. neatly bound.

"We never in all our experience met with a more interesting work, and one breathing more fully and firmly the very essence of Christian philanthropy and national patriotism, and that too in the most simple and unambitious language, as if the writer were not aware of his power of influencing all the better feelings of the human heart."—*Literary Chronicle.*

"This volume reminds us forcibly of that most delightful of all biographies, 'The Doctor,' to which indeed it is little if at all inferior."—*Britannia.*

"It is the pious offering of one who may be deemed a proper follower in the footsteps of that good man, Legh Richmond."—*Argus.*

MORTAL LIFE; AND THE STATE OF THE SOUL AFTER DEATH;

CONFORMABLE TO DIVINE REVELATION. By ALEXANDER COPLAND, Esq., Author of "The Existence of Other Worlds," &c. In one thick vol. 8vo., price 15s. bound.

"The work will afford in perusal, to all sorrowing relations, the consolation and diversion of mind of the most congenial kind. It neither leads the thoughts to dwell painfully on one idea—that of loss—nor does it altogether withdraw the mind from its contemplation: an effort still more painful. The study of a work like this, on the contrary, while it gradually weans grief from its melancholy occupation, supplies it with the sweetest and most cheerful of all balm—the happy certainty of re-union, not after the lapse of vast ages of time, but at the instant term of mortal existence."—*Theological Review.*

A HISTORY OF THE CHURCH OF CHRIST.

In a Course of Lectures. By the Rev. CHARLES MACKENZIE, A.M., Vicar of St. Helen's, Bishopsgate, and Head Master of Queen Elizabeth's Grammar School, St. Olave's, Southwark. In one vol. post 8vo., price 8s. 6d. neatly bound in cloth.

"Although the author is able and earnest, he is not bigoted or intolerant."—*Literary Gazette.*

"It is but an octavo, yet within its conveniently compendious pages it contains a review carefully taken of the progress of the Church of Christ, through all the perils of persecution, dissent, and heresy, by which it has been tried as in a furnace, up to its confirmed establishment in this country at the epoch of 1688."—*Herald.*

THE IDEAL OF THE ENGLISH CHURCH.

A Sketch. By the Rev. R. MONTGOMERY, M.A., Author of "Luther," "The Gospel before the Age," &c. &c. 8vo., price 2s. 6d. sewed.

A NEW SPELLING-BOOK OF THE ENGLISH LANGUAGE.

Containing all the Monosyllables; a copious Selection of Polysyllables, carefully arranged and accented; Progressive Lessons, chiefly from the Holy Scriptures; a List of Words of various Meanings; a short Bible Catechism; Questions on Scripture History; and School Prayers. By J. S. MOORE, Master of the Brewers' Company's School. 12mo., price 1s. 6d. bound.

ARITHMETIC UNVEILED:

Being a Series of Tables and Rules, whereby most of the calculations in business may be either mentally performed, or so abridged as to save half the time usually employed. To which are annexed a Multiplication Table extending to 200 times 200, and Tables of Interest on an improved plan. The whole adapted to the use of both the first merchant and the most humble trader. By JAMES MCDOWALL, Accountant. In demy 12mo., price 5s. bound in cloth.

THE GRAMMARIAN;

Or, THE ENGLISH WRITER AND SPEAKER'S ASSISTANT: comprising SHALL and WILL made easy to Foreigners, with instances of their Misuse on the Part of the Natives of England. Also SCOTTICISMS, designed to correct Improprieties of Speech and Writing. By JAMES BEATTIE, LL.D. 24mo., price 2s. cloth boards.

A SYSTEM OF ARITHMETIC,

With the PRINCIPLES OF LOGARITHMS. Compiled for Merchant Taylors' School. By RICHARD FREDERICK CLARKE, Teacher. Third Edition, demy 12mo., price 3s. bound.

"The great object attained in this excellent work is a most judicious abridgment of the labour of teaching and learning every branch of Arithmetic, by rendering the Rules and Explanations so very simple and intelligible, that the study becomes a pleasure instead of a task, to the youthful pupil."

Poetry.

RHYMES AND RECOLLLECTIONS OF A HAND-LOOM WEAVER.

By WILLIAM THOM, of Inverury, Aberdeenshire. Third Edition, with a Portrait. Post 8vo., price 4s. An Edition on large paper, 8vo., price 7s. 6d.

"An' syne whan nichts grew cauld and lang
Ae while he sicht—ae while he sang."—*Old Ballad.*

"The Rhymes are to be read with interest, and not without admiration."
Examiner.

"Let every good man and woman think of the author: from this book he looks for some consolation, and we trust it will bring him still more effectual protection from other sources."—*Literary Gazette.*

THE COTTAR'S SUNDAY, AND OTHER POEMS,

Chiefly in the Scottish Dialect. By PETER STILL. In fcap. 8vo., price 3s. cloth.

THE PALACE OF FANTASY; OR THE BARD'S IMAGERY.

WITH OTHER POEMS. By J. S. HARDY, Author of "Hours of Thought; or, Poetic Musings." In fcap. 8vo., price 3s. 6d. cloth.

"There is much of the pure gold of poetry in this handsome little volume."—*Macclesfield Chronicle.*

"The principal poem in this little volume, written in the Spenserian Stanza and diction, contains many pleasing passages. . . . Much talent is evinced by the author."—*Oxford Herald.*

"This poem contains many passages which one would read again after the first perusal—a remark which cannot be made of much of the poetry which is published. Some of the miscellaneous poems are very sweet, reminding one of Cowper's smaller poems."—*Herts County Press.*

"The 'Palace of Fantasy' is of a higher character than the generality of poems: the spirit of poetry is perceptible throughout, and the work has a healthy tone and purpose."—*Cheltenham Journal.*

"This little volume is one of considerable merit. The principal poem contains many beautiful passages, original and striking, which cannot fail to please."—*Plymouth Herald.*

"Mr. Hardy has produced a poem which, had it appeared during the last century, would have secured for him a sure place among the British Poets."—*Derbyshire Chron.*

A METRICAL VERSION OF THE SONG OF SOLOMON,

AND OTHER POEMS. By A LATE GRADUATE OF OXFORD. In fcap. 8vo., price 4s. 6d. cloth.

KING RENE'S DAUGHTER.

A Lyrical Drama. From the Danish of HENRIK HERTZ. By JANE FRANCIS CHAPMAN, Translator of "Waldemar," and "King Eric and the Outlaw." In fcap. 8vo., price 2s. 6d. cloth.

ISLAFORD, AND OTHER POEMS.

A Book for Winter Evenings and Summer Moods. By GEORGE MURRAY. In fcap. 8vo., price 4s. cloth.

THE COLUMBIAD:

Comprising Geographical Sketches, and a Narrative of Nautical Adventures in the Eastern Seas, including the perils of a storm, and providential escape from shipwreck: with Meditations on a Future State. By ARCHIBALD TUCKER RITCHIE, Esq. In demy 8vo., price 10s. handsomely bound in cloth.

"Under this title the author has given a poetical narrative of his voyage in the Indian Ocean, somewhat in the manner of 'Falconer's Shipwreck.' .... The most remarkable passage is that where he announces a new attempt to explain the phenomena of Geology in connexion with the first chapter of Genesis. . . . We would recommend the perusal of this poem, which contains some pretty passages both to interest and instruct the reader."—*Edinburgh Weekly Journal.*

"This is an interesting poem. .... In so far as it is descriptive, it is a painting from Nature, and a narrative of real life. The author can say, 'All which I saw, and part of which I was.' If to landsmen the poem is interesting, it must be peculiarly so to those 'whose march is on the deep.' .... The author is evidently a person of right principles, of a kind and pious heart, and of a generous and polished mind. .... He has a higher object than merely giving pleasure; he seeks to benefit his readers."
Scottish Guardian.

DAYS IN THE EAST:

A Poem in Two Cantos. Descriptive of Scenery in India, the Departure from Home, the Voyage and subsequent Career of an Officer in the East India Company's Army. By JAMES HENRY BURKE, Esq., of Marble Hill, Lieutenant Bombay Engineers, Member of the Bombay Branch of Royal Asiatic Society. In demy 8vo., price 6s. bound.

"The stanzas of Mr. Burke bespeak at once high feeling, a vigorous cultivated intelligence, and a delicate poetic taste."—*Morning Herald.*
"The execution is even, finished, and good."—*Weekly Chronicle.*

Embellished Works and Prints.

THE BYRON GALLERY:

A Series of thirty-six Historical Embellishments, illustrating the Poetical Works of LORD BYRON; beautifully engraved from Original Drawings and Paintings by Sir Thomas Lawrence, P.R.A., H. Howard, R.A., A. E. Chalon, R.A., J. Stothard, R.A., R. Westall, R.A., and other eminent Artists: adapted, by their size and excellence, to bind up with and embellish every edition published in England of LORD BYRON'S WORKS, and also the various sizes and editions published in France, Germany, and America. Price 12s. elegantly bound, forming a splendid ornament for the drawing-room table.

STANFIELD'S COAST SCENERY:

A Series of Picturesque Views in the British Channel and on the Coast of France. From Original Drawings, taken expressly for the work, by CLARKSON STANFIELD, Esq., R.A. Second edition. Forty plates engraved in line, in the most finished style, with descriptive letterpress. One volume 8vo., handsomely bound in cloth, gilt edges. Price 12s.

ILLUSTRATIONS TO "ADVENTURE IN NEW ZEALAND."

By Edward Jerningham Wakefield, Esq. Lithographed from Original Drawings taken on the spot, by Mrs. Wicksteed, Miss King, Mrs. Fox, Mr. John Saxton, Mr. Charles Heaphy, Mr. S. C. Brees, and Captain W. Mein Smith, R.N. One volume folio, with fifteen Plates, including Views of Port Nicholson, Wellington, Nelson, Petre, New Plymouth, and other Settlements; with Portraits of Native Chiefs, and their Dwellings; and Drawings of Trees and Plants. Price 3l. 3s. plain; 4l. 14s. 6d. coloured.

"Drawn with great skill, and exceedingly well lithographed; their great value consists in their giving correct representations of the scenes and objects they depict."—*Atlas.*

MADEIRA ILLUSTRATED.

A series of Eight Views, drawn from Nature, and on Stone by Andrew Picken. With a Map, and a description of the Island. Edited by Dr. James Macauley, M.A., Imperial folio, price 2l. 2s. plain; 4l. 4s. coloured.

THE ORIENTAL PORTFOLIO:

A Series of splendid Illustrations of the Scenery, Antiquities, Architecture, Manners, Costumes, &c. of the East. From original Sketches in the collections of Lord William Bentinck, K.C.B., Captain R. M. Grindlay, Lady Wilmot Horton, Sir Henry Willock, K.L.S., Thomas Bacon, Esq., James Baillie Fraser, Esq., and other travellers. The Literary Department of the Work by Horace H. Wilson, Esq., M.A., F.R.S., &c. &c. The series is now completed, comprising eleven beautifully finished Plates, tinted in imitation of Drawings. Price 2l. 2s. elegantly bound in large folio.

The object of this undertaking is to supply what has long been felt to be a desideratum; namely, Graphic Illustrations of the Scenery, Antiquities, Architecture, Manners, Costumes, &c. of the East, which, as the theatre of so many brilliant military achievements, and such extensive commercial enterprise, is daily increasing in interest with the British public. The Drawings for the work are made by the first Artists in the Kingdom, from the Original Sketches taken on the spot.

A GENERAL VIEW OF THE FALLS OF NIAGARA.

Etched in the best manner, on Copper. By F. C. Lewis, Esq., Engraver to the Queen. From a Drawing made on the spot, by Captain James Graham, of H. M. 70th Regiment. On an extended scale of forty-three by nineteen inches. Price, India Proofs, 2l. 2s.; Plain Prints, 15s.; beautifully coloured as Drawings, 21s.

The view embraces the two Falls, including Goat Island and the country on both banks of the river; and presents a faithful and complete picture of this majestic scene.

ILLUSTRATIONS OF FRIENDSHIP'S OFFERING.

A few Proof Impressions of the varied and beautiful designs illustrative of the several volumes of this elegant Annual, particularly suited for ornamenting Albums and Scrapbooks, may be had separately.

Price, India proofs, 2s. 6d. each; plain prints 1s. each.

PORTRAITS OF EMINENT AUTHORS AND ACTRESSES.

PORTRAITS of the following eminent AUTHORS and ACTRESSES, engraved in line from Original Drawings, of a size suitable for Illustration, may be had at 1s. each, prints; and 2s. 6d. each, India proofs.

THOMAS CARLYLE, Esq.
CHARLES DICKENS, Esq.
WILLIAM WORDSWORTH, Esq.
ALFRED TENNYSON, Esq.
ROBERT BROWNING, Esq.
ANDREW STEINMETZ, Esq.
MISS HARRIET MARTINEAU.

MRS. NESBITT.
MISS HELEN FAUCIT.
MISS ELLEN TREE.
MADAME VESTRIS.
MISS ADELAIDE KEMBLE.
MISS O'NEIL.
MISS FOOTE.
MISS BRUNTON.

ARIEL. Designed by E. T. PARRIS, finely engraved in line by F. BACON. Proofs 15s., prints 10s.

THE SMUGGLER'S ESCAPE. Painted by H. W. HARVEY. Engraved by C. ROSENBERG. Plain 5s., coloured 10s. 6d.

A Marine picture, representing the chase of a smuggling lugger by a Frigate, taken from a scene in Mr. James's Novel "The Smuggler."

VIEW OF MELBOURNE, PORT PHILIP. Painted by W. F. LIARDET. Engraved by J. W. LOWRY. With Index-plate, price 10s. 6d.

In this View every public and private building of importance is represented with minute accuracy, and referred to by name in the Index-plate; the foreground being animated by characteristic groups of natives, &c. The plate is published under the auspices of the Superintendent and principal residents of Melbourne.

VIEWS IN CALCUTTA. By JAMES B. FRASER, Esq. Engraved in Aquatint, and beautifully coloured from nature. Price 10s. 6d.

These Views embrace the principal edifices of Calcutta, and represent the streets, squares, promenades, and suburbs of this splendid city, filled with the motley groups of Europeans and Natives; the river and shipping being also shown under atmospheric effects characteristic of the climate and country.

VIEWS OF SETTLEMENTS IN NEW ZEALAND :—

VIEW OF WELLINGTON, NEW ZEALAND. Plain 3s., coloured 5s.
VIEW OF LAMBTON HARBOUR, NEW ZEALAND. Plain 3s., coloured 5s.
VIEW OF NEW PLYMOUTH, NEW ZEALAND. Plain 3s., coloured 5s.
VIEW OF MOUNT EGMONT, NEW ZEALAND. Plain 3s., coloured 5s.

These Views are faithful representations of the features of those parts of the coast of New Zealand selected as sites of the Company's principal settlements. They were taken by Mr. Charles Heaphy, Draughtsman to the New Zealand Company, and exhibit the appearance of the country under the influence of colonization; showing the first habitations of the settlers, and the dawnings of commerce and civilization on a savage state. They are executed in tinted Lithography by Mr. Allom.

VIEWS OF ALL THE PRINCIPAL TOWNS IN SCOTLAND. Each, coloured, 7s. 6d.

WORKS PUBLISHED BY SMITH, ELDER AND CO.

MAPS AND CHARTS:—

A NEW MAP OF THE PUNJAUB. Coloured 1s.; in case 1s. 6d.

ARROWSMITH'S MAP OF AUSTRALIA AND NEW ZEALAND. In sheets, coloured, 1s. 6d.; in case, coloured, 2s. 6d.

ARROWSMITH'S MAP OF NEW ZEALAND. In sheets, coloured, 1s. 6d.; in case, coloured, 2s. 6d.

CHART OF COOK'S STRAITS, NEW ZEALAND. By CHARLES HEAPHY, Esq. Price 8s.

HEIGHTS OF ALL THE MOUNTAINS IN THE WORLD. Plain 1s., coloured 2s.

PARBURY'S MAP OF OVERLAND ROUTE TO INDIA. In case 8s., in sheets, 6s.

BOOKS FOR THE USE OF THE BLIND.

Printed with a very distinct Raised Roman Letter, adapted to their Touch.

The HOLY BIBLE, in 15 vols. 4to. bound. Any volume separately:—

	£	s.	d.
Vol. 1. Genesis	0	9	0
— 2. Exodus and Leviticus	0	13	0
— 3. Numbers	0	9	0
— 4. Deuteronomy	0	7	6
— 5. Joshua, Judges, and Ruth	0	10	0
— 6. Samuel	0	11	0
— 7. Kings	0	11	0
— 8. Chronicles	0	11	0
— 9. Job, Ezra, and Nehemiah	0	9	0
— 10. Psalms	0	13	0
— 11. Proverbs, Ecclesiastes, Song of Solomon and Esther	0	8	6
— 12. Isaiah	0	10	6
— 13. Jeremiah and Lamentations	0	11	0
— 14. Ezekiel	0	10	0
— 15. Daniel, to the end	0	11	0
The NEW TESTAMENT, complete, 4 vols. bound	2	0	0
The Four Gospels, separately:—			
Matthew	0	5	6
Mark	0	4	0
Luke	0	5	6
John	0	4	6
The Acts of the Apostles	0	5	6
The Epistles to the Ephesians and Galatians	0	3	0
The Church of England Catechism	0	1	0
Church of Scotland Shorter Catechism	0	2	6
Selections from Eminent Authors	0	1	6
Selections of Sacred Poetry, with Tunes	0	2	0
Arithmetical Boards	0	10	6
Map of England and Wales	0	2	0
Ruth and James	0	2	6
Report and Statement of Education	0	2	0
Specimens of Printing Type	0	2	6
First and Second Book of Lessons	0	2	0
A Selection of Æsop's Fables, with Woodcuts	0	2	0
Lessons on Natural Religion	0	1	6
The Psalms and Paraphrases, 2 vols.	0	16	0
The Morning and Evening Services	0	2	6
The History of the Bible	0	2	0
Musical Catechism, with Tunes	0	3	6
English Grammar	0	5	0
Tod's Lectures, vols. 1 and 2, each	0	2	6
Description of London, by Chambers	0	3	0
Meditations on the Sacrament	0	4	0

www.ingramcontent.com/pod-product-compliance
Lightning Source LLC
Chambersburg PA
CBHW080434110426
42743CB00016B/3167